FOREWORD

In *The Way of the Black Star* Tony J. Br
approach to the understanding of 'the wა
for everyone, male or female, young an
sound foundation for the beginner.

The text is clear and concise and the key
by-step photographs, guiding the student systematically through a
learning programme designed around the points of the star. It covers all
aspects of teaching and martial technique and above all explains the
underlying philosophy and values which are the basis of Aikido.

Anyone interested in martial arts will find this book fascinating, it is an
essential guide for all Aikido students.

Sensei Terry D Bayliss

The Way of the Black Star

AIKIDO BASICS

黑星道

The Way of the Black Star

AIKIDO BASICS

TONY J. BROWN

The Pentland Press
Edinburgh Cambridge Durham USA

First published in 1997
by The Pentland Press Ltd.
Hutton Close
South Church
Bishop Auckland
Durham

ISBN : 1 85821 503 X

Typeset, Printed and Bound by
Lintons Printers, County Durham.

A I K I D O

A I } *Harmony Unification* 合

K I } *Spirit, Life, Energy* 気

D O } *A Way* 道

The Way Of The Harmonious Spirit

ACKNOWLEDGEMENT

I wish to thank Sensei Terry D. Bayliss
for his help and guidance throughout my
Aikido studies.

T.J.B.

INTRODUCTION

Black Star Aikido offers the newcomer to this art the opportunity to study the traditional aspects of Aikido whilst placing emphasis on developing good martial art skills. As with all the traditional martial arts, Black Star's first objective is self-defence. A martial system that is not sufficient to maintain this objective is structurally weak. It could be likened to an expensive top of the range car which has no fuel. It may appear impressive yet its primary purpose of motion is not served, and therefore it is of limited use.

The student is advised to follow this manual systematically. First study the text, then practise softly and slowly. Correct repetition breeds correct practice.

Take time to understand each movement before moving on to the next. Even though this manual only shows the actions from one side, it is strongly recommended that the attacks and defences be practised both left and right handed. The whole body must react equally when attacked from any direction. In reality one's opponent may attack by striking left or right handed, so train equally and the First Objective is maintained.

By taking each page, one step at a time the Aikido novice will soon be engrossed with the power and beauty this unique discipline has to offer.

Sensei Tony J. Brown

FIRST OBJECTIVE — SELF DEFENCE

CONTENTS

The Way Of The Black Star

Each point of the star represents the different elements used in the training and understanding of Aikido. When all the points are linked together, the outer circle becomes one with the star. In essence, this perfect union of two entities is Aikido.

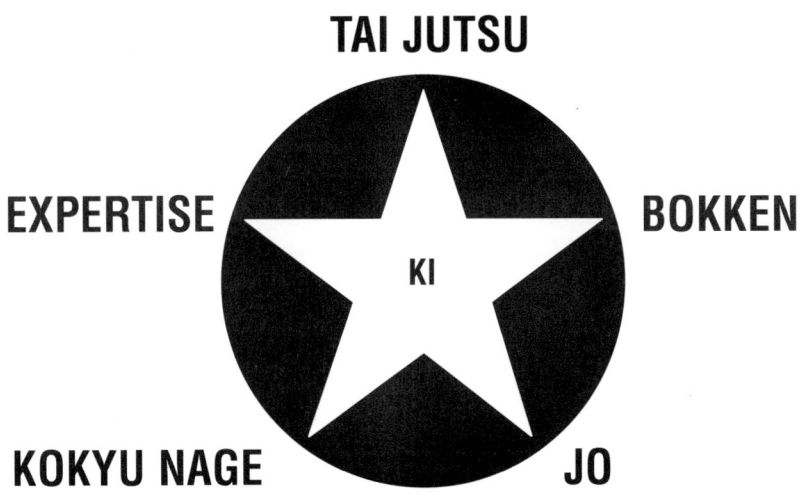

TAI JUTSU

EXPERTISE   **BOKKEN**

KI

KOKYU NAGE   **JO**

Tai Jutsu....   The use of the body. Empty handed techniques applied to all forms of attack. The beginning of the circle.

Bokken....   Wooden sword. A training aid, to assist understanding.

Jo....   Wooden staff. A training aid, to assist understanding.

Kokyu Nage...   A type of throw employing no joint technique.

Expertise.....   Martial skills applied where necessary.

Ki....   Inner energy, emitted from the central point.

Aikido - Martial Art

In order to understand what a martial art actually is this term will be dissected into its two parts:

Martial: This means warlike, military, fighting.

Art: Art refers to any specific skill or application.

Hence the term martial art refers to any fighting discipline, any group of skills used for the training for combat and survival. Primarily a martial art is for self-defence. It is not a sport, or a keep fit activity or a social engagement. A martial art may encompass these attributes but its initial purpose is the most important.

What is Self -Defence?

Each and every one of us has the right to control how close we wish for another person to enter into our 'space'. People of a shy nature will naturally distance themselves to a position that feels safe and comfortable. This placing of one's body in a position of safety and security is in essence, self defence. Once the option of walking away has been eliminated then a more physical means of regaining one's space is necessary.

Through serious practice of a martial art one's space may be controlled more fully. The normal accepted area allotted for one's own individual space is approximately as follows:

Spread both arms at shoulder level outwards to the sides of the body. Stretch the fingertips. Keeping both feet in the same area turn the body around full circle (360°). Imagine drawing a line with the fingertips in the air. The circle scribed dictates one's space. This may be known as a 'Circle of Confidence'. This circle may be increased in size as one's awareness develops. Thus when a potential aggressor comes within this space it may be intuitively acknowledged.

Aikido - A Martial Art Discipline

Within the practice of any group activity the role of keeping order is very important. Good order within the unit allows one to feel in a safe and controlled environment. As the practice of a martial art uses varied measures of physical contact, the control of both the individual and the collective is even more important. The unit discipline will achieve a good base from which the individual may achieve a high standard of personal discipline.

Dojo Etiquette - Club Politeness:
The following rules act as a base to which all Aikido societies adhere:

1 A Standing Bow is made on entering the training hall. The word *Rei* is Japanese for the bow. Also upon exiting the *Dojo*, one must bow.

2 Wait for permission from the Instructor to enter onto the mat or into the training area. This is a safety factor. Remember the Instructor is responsible for the well-being of every student. The Instructor should be addressed by the title of *Sensei*, which is Japanese for teacher. It is the equivalent of calling a teacher Sir in western minds, but this title of *Sensei* also applies to female instructors. Some schools also regard all black belts as *Sensei* as a term of respect even though they may not be actually teaching that particular class. Black belts in Aikido wear what is called, a *Hakama*, skirtlike trousers, usually in black. This is also a traditional Japanese item of clothing.

3 Bow to one's partner before and after practice. If training with a higher grade, then they will initiate the *rei*.

4 If for any reason one wishes to leave the training area before the set finishing time of the class, then permission should be sought from the *Sensei*. This is so students are not just stepping into and out of the *Dojo* whenever they feel like it. It is a controlled environment for learning, not a playground.

5 Although safety factors will be given to the new students upon arriving at the Dojo for the first time, it is worth bearing in mind that jewellery must be removed, including earrings, watches etc. before practice commences. In the case of wedding rings most schools will allow for them to be taped around so they are safe to be worn during practice. Students wearing spectacles are advised by Sensei.

Some phrases that may be used by the Sensei are listed so one may become familiar with them and their meaning:

Hajime:	Begin
Keiko:	Practice
Yame:	Stop
Seiza:	Formal sitting posture on both knees

Counting One to Ten

1   *Ichi*

2   *Ni*

3   *San*

4   *Shi/Yon*

5   *Go*

6   *Roku*

7   *Shitch/Nana*

8   *Hachi*

9   *Ku*

10 *Ju*

If one has any doubts about the commands of the *Sensei*, simply ask a higher grade than oneself if a minor question, or politely ask the *Sensei*. It is worthy to note that whilst one may consider the teacher is there to teach you, thus putting the responsibility of teaching onto the teacher, it is also worth remembering that one is there to learn: the responsibility of learning is on the student. This is how it should be. These simple phrases will stand in good stead a student who is eager to learn :

IF IN DOUBT   ASK SENSEI

A True Student of Aikido Receives Knowledge Others Expect It To Be Given.

What is Aikido?

Aikido is a martial art that incorporates techniques originally based on ancient Jujitsu with body throwing techniques and movements. It seeks to utilise an opponent's power and either blend with it or redirect it in order to apply joint locks or throwing techniques. The use of strength in this discipline is not an initial factor. One does not need to develop large biceps and a strong fist, but needs to acquire the overall body power that is derived when the actions of the body are unified with the power of the mind and eventually a deep spiritual awareness of the self. The elements that make Aikido unique lie within its training, its underlying principles and its philosophy. Combining these three factors one not only develops the skilful use of this martial art but also one's own character and mental awareness.

The Principles of Aikido

Aikido seeks a way to " blend with one's opponent". This phrase is often used in the teaching of Aikido and is often interpreted as a soft, nice way of dealing with a potential assailant. This is not strictly so. 'To blend' simply means to go the same way, to harmonise and be in tune with the forces and environment. When driving a car onto a motorway it is important that the speed and direction of the existing traffic is matched in order to join in and carry onward safely. A reduction in speed or a change of direction would act as a block. In Aikido one never blocks. Below are listed some simple phrases that embody Aikido principles. Whilst they may be not completely understood at this point one may revise this page and grasp their meaning easily after practising this art.

The Principles of Aikido:

When pushed	..	TURN		Back to Basics
When pulled	...	ENTER		Spin to Win
Go with the	..	FLOW		
A Greater Force re-directed is ... NEUTRALISED				
Power Through Movement				

CONTROL IS POWER
Always seek to manipulate the opponent's power to gain total control.

CIRCULAR POWER

Aikido uses natural circular and spiral motions to employ the various joint locks and throwing motions. Performing movements in straight lines or directly up or down may require more strength than by using a circular path. The rotation of the hips, shoulders and head all enhance this circular motion. If one takes a square piece of cardboard and places a pin directly at its centre and spins it continuously then it appears to become a circle. This rotation blends away the square, sharp, right angled edges, into a soft movable curve. If one has the skill to apply this same principle to an opponent, then by attacking the central point and applying a circular motion the jagged forces are dispersed into a sphere that may be more easily dealt with. With this idea in mind it is important to be aware that the central point of oneself (2 inches below the navel) must be solidly based in order to apply good techniques that may not be countered or uprooted. It will be seen that the practice of Aikido weaponry will enhance the *basing of one's centre*.

Aikido - Managing Force

To obtain a clear picture of exactly how one wishes to deal with an aggressor's attacking force / energy / assault, some simple equations show these principles of Force Management:

AIKIDO NEVER MEETS FORCE WITH FORCE

Attacking Force   Defending Force

$$\longrightarrow \quad \longleftarrow$$

Stalemate

THE STRONGEST FORCE WILL WIN

WINNER   LOSER

$$\longrightarrow \quad \longleftarrow$$

The practice of Aikido desires to achieve a situation that allows the defender to be able to manage a greater force directed at them without exerting the same effort in retaliation. Obviously, a weaker person needs an equation that does not meet this potential attacking force head on.

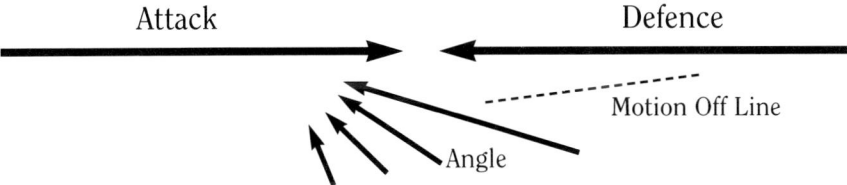

The defender moves off the line of attack and applies his force at the correct ANGLE to the attacking force, by technique.

Aikido utilises body movements to absorb, re-direct, amplify or simply escape the initial attacking force of the assailant. At first one learns with limited movements so as not to confuse the issues of studying the basic mechanics of technique. After a time the Aikidoka (student of Aikido) may begin to perform the same tasks by using more body motions and body flow, enhancing many aspects of this art.

POWER THROUGH MOVEMENT

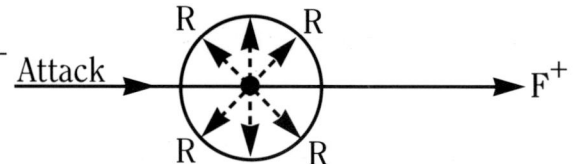

RE-DIRECTION OF FORCE : R
CONTINUATION OF FLOW OF FORCE : F
STUDENT'S POSITION : ●

Not only does the Aikidoka learn how to accept the oncoming attacking force, but also how to deal with the negative intentions of this force. The mind and body, through correct education and practice learn NOT to get negatively involved with this situation but allow it to pass through them, turning it into a positive state that may be utilised in the technique.

CHANNELLING NEGATIVE INTO POSITIVE ACTION

The Founder of Aikido - Morihei Ueshiba

The Man - The Art

On the 14th December 1883, Morihei Ueshiba was born. From an early age he began the study of Japanese Budo (martial ways). With such devotion and after years of arduous training, Ueshiba became an accomplished master in several styles of Ju-jitsu, Kendo (sword arts) and Sojitsu (spear combat). The lead up to the development of Aikido as we know it today, was to take Ueshiba many years in the perfection of his ideas. It can be seen that these arts and Ueshiba's expert foundation in the fighting arts were to be a good base from which to experiment and develop Aikido.

Once Master Ueshiba had reached excellence as a warrior, then his religious beliefs began to question the 'need to defeat' one's opponent. From this point on the messages being practised were to become Aikido. Rather than meeting force with force, Aikido turns the attacking force and momentum back onto the opponent, in a technique utilising circular and spiral motion. By no means is this a passive art, but rather a martial art that allows one to become victorious over the attacker and finally winning over the self. This makes Aikido ideal for women and persons of less aggressive nature. Strength has no place within this art. Master Ueshiba, known as 'O Sensei' which means great teacher to his students, left his legacy to the rest of the world in the hope that we may use the teachings to bring peace and inner calmness to our way of lives. Nothing is achieved by those who sit back and let others sort their problems out. If one is prepared to train in the right spirit for the right reasons, then the art of Aikido will surely flourish.

Morihei Ueshiba .. 1883 - 1969

Information for the New Student

What to Wear?

In order to practise safely, the new student to this martial art is recommended to dress in the traditional uniform known as a Gi. This consists of a jacket, trousers and, to start with, a white or red belt. This uniform will be made in white cotton canvas and may vary in thickness and quality depending on how much is paid. Most martial art Dojos (clubs) will allow new students at first to practise in a track-suit or jogging suit, anything clean and tidy looking that will allow for free and comfortable movement.

Many new students in their first week of joining a club wish to purchase the Gi immediately so they may feel more at ease with the rest of the members already kitted out in white uniforms. This may prove costly at first as there are fees to the club that may need to be paid in the initial few weeks, including insurance fees. It is advisable to wait until the student has definitely decided to continue with this particular activity.

Age and Fitness?

Although one may practise Aikido well into old age the majority of schools will insist that new persons wishing to begin training in this activity, obtain their doctor's approval i.e. Persons of over 45 years of age. This is for their well being and own peace of mind.

As fitness levels are concerned the novice will start off slowly at his own pace and gradually with time and practice the fitness level will improve. This will not only help with their Aikido training but will improve the quality of daily life.

Warming Up

Before the practice of any martial art or any demanding physical activity, the Instructor or the person taking charge will make sure that all students have undergone a thorough warm up procedure. The purpose of the warm up is to prepare the body and mind for the activity that is to commence. By completing a thorough warm up the body is in a much safer state to endure the forthcoming physical hardships. This will help prevent the injury of cold and unprepared muscle tissue. The mind will also feel at ease and ready to accept information.

Programme A

This warm up programme has been designed so that individuals may pace themselves. Either alone or in a class students may perform this routine in respect of their own fitness level and will not feel any pressure to keep up with the advanced students. A black belt would complete the same programme but would be expected to have repeated more of the exercises within the same time frame. Depending on how hard or how fast one wishes to train then this routine allows for personal development.

Programme A incorporates the following elements within its warm up:
Raising the overall body temperature
Raising the pulse rate
Fitness training
Endurance/ Stamina training
Taking the body parts through their natural spectrum of movements
Mind readiness

New students are always advised to complete the exercises to their own capabilities, slowly and cautiously at first, paying particular attention to breathing, deeply and methodically.

This programme has 10 exercises. It is suggested that each set of exercises takes approximately 15 - 25 seconds, or in the cases of sets 5,6,7 repetitions of 10. Obviously this is only a guideline and may be changed accordingly.

1 Running on the Spot
2 Alternate Hand to Knee
3 Hip Turning (turning loosely on the spot)
4 Gathering Sand
5 Press Ups
6 Squat Thrusts
7 Sit Ups
8 Running on the Spot
9 Shoulder Rotations (swinging both arms up and over the head continuously: forwards then backward directions)
10 Hip Turning

Repeat Programme
Whilst sets 1,3,5,6,7,8,9,10 are self explanatory sets 2 and 4 are specified below:

Programme A: Alternate Hand to Knee
After running on the spot the body will have become increasingly warmer and will feel ready to take the arms and legs through their natural range of movements.

Stand naturally, feet approximately shoulder width apart. Stretch the left hand up and outwards to the left side of the body, pointing eagerly to the ceiling to make for good arm, shoulder and surrounding muscle stretch.

As the left hand travels down, across the front of the body, the right knee comes up to the centre of the body in order to meet the hand. Contact is made with the edge of the hand upon the inside of the knee, or inner thigh area. Replace this leg after contact.

The right hand points up and out towards the right side of the body and as before is brought down across the front of the body to make contact with the opposite raising knee/thigh.
Replace this leg after contact.
REPEAT MANY TIMES

Gathering Sand Exercise:
This is a descriptive name, as one can visualise bending down to cup the sand in both hands, then by raising the legs and arms upwards, throw the sand up and outwards over the head.

Stand naturally facing forward. Keeping the arms on the inside of both legs, bend the knees to lower the body down so that the hands may travel down to reach the floor. Keep the back straight. In a cupping motion, with both palms open, imagine gathering as much sand as one can in the two hands. Naturally the hands will come together crossing over one another, in a circular manner.

Straighten up the legs whilst bringing both hands up in front of the body and throw the arms up and outwards above the head. Visualise the sand being scattered both above oneself and at a distance away.

At the final point of the movement, the body should be in an uplifted state momentarily, if possible rise up onto the toes. Extend the arms and fingers. This will make for a good overall body stretch.

REPEAT MANY TIMES

Light Stretching

After the completion of the above it is advisable to perform some light stretching exercises, whilst the body is warm and supple. As specific stretches will be demonstrated by the Instructor for the new students, some simple guidelines are given:

The stretching of any part of the body must be done slowly and cautiously.

Avoid bouncing or applying added weight. This should only be done for advanced types of stretching where one needs added stimulus to improve. The newcomer will suffice with natural stretches.

Pain is the brain's way of informing the body that something is too extreme, avoid painful stretches. Obviously there may be a little discomfort in taking some of the rarely used body parts through some of the exercises, so common sense must prevail. We are individuals with different grades of flexibility so do not attempt to position yourself in a way that appears to be comfortable for someone else.

Upon finishing this programme perform either Partner Tai Sabaki practice or Mirroring Exercise. This will introduce the practice of movement, sensitivity and blending with one's partner, the key elements that are to become integral throughout one's Aikido training. Hands on practice with some of the other students, whilst still in a relaxed frame of mind will allow a safe and at ease feeling to be carried through for the execution of technique.

Mirroring Exercise - Sensitivity Drill

The following exercise is a simple way of illustrating how important it is to be sensitive enough to feel your partner's movements and balance and be able either to re-direct or overthrow them to one's own advantage. It is a beneficial exercise to practise in order to achieve a good awareness of how the balance of both persons changes rapidly from many angles, both in the attack and defence modes. It also enhances one's own personal stability through toning up the leg, toe, hip muscles etc, and at the same time teaching the necessity for fluid and interchangeable motion.

As in the photograph below:
Stand facing one's partner square on. The distance should be sufficient to enable both persons to place the palms of both hands on the opposite person's shoulders.

Contact palms of both hands with the partner's. From this position either person may move in any way or manner they feel is best to make the partner lose balance and therefore take a step. The first person to move a foot from the original start position loses. Naturally start again. Whilst it is not strictly a competition, but done for the beneficial learning factors as described, it should be borne in mind that as a stimulus for getting better and not to be uplifted or overthrown so easily next time round, it is enough in itself. At first much strength is used but as practice experience accumulates then one learns the added options of being able to work softly and with a little subtlety.

To make for varied practice on this theme both partners may lock the fingers of each hand which gives a new set of variables, as now one may pull and lock onto the partner, to either resist or destroy the situation.

Kiba-dachi (commonly known as Horse-Stance)

This stance is used in many martial arts and is ideal for this exercise. A position in which the legs are spread approximately twice the width of the shoulders, the body weight is evenly distributed and the toes are pointed straight forward, also referred to as a "Straddle Leg Stance"

Tai Jutsu

A Flower's Beauty Lies Within Its Seed
Rooted Deep, It Finds Its Way

Tai Jutsu
Evolution - The Learning Process

The practice of Aikido can be categorised into three levels. Each level may be thought of as a building block, progressively building upon itself. The initial block is the most important, therefore much time and effort will be spent in training to allow this to become a solid foundation from which one may advance further. The pyramid below shows the three levels:

1 **Kihon** - Basic form of technique. Solid, step by step movement. The initial level of learning, the roots.
2 **Ki No Nagare** - Fluid form of technique, flowing movements, its branches.
3 **Kokyu-ho** - The manifestation of internal energy through movement, mastery of technique. The final level of unification of the self, mind, body and spirit acting as one. Blossoming its flowers.

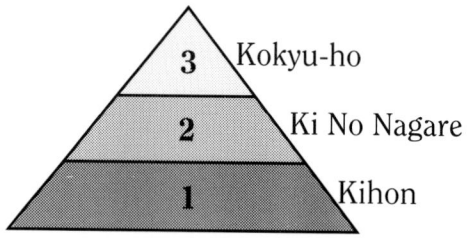

Rather than specify a technique and explain how it is performed at each level, a simple comparison will show this progression:

1 **Ice** - Solid form of technique - H_2O
2 **Water** - Fluid form of technique - H_2O. It is important to note that whilst the shape and characterisation of the H_2O has changed, it is still H_2O. Its principle elements remain identical. The technique changes form but not its principles.
3 **Steam** - Transparent form. Able to move freely.

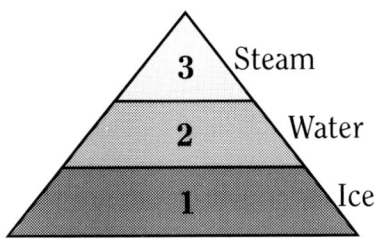

It can now be understood that a technique is first learnt in basic form, then with much practice may be evolved forward to the next levels.

HARD	SOFT
static	motion
basic	creative
identical	unique/individual

Tai Jutsu
Methods of Practising

Method

Tai-jutsu is the way in which techniques are applied to one's opponent by the empty hands. Once the ability to perform a specific technique or movement has been achieved then these skills may be translated to other methods of practice. In Aikido there are three methods in the way one wishes to practise:

1 **Tachi Waza** ... Attack and defence executed from standing positions. The most common form of practice.

2 **Hanmi handachi Waza** ... The attacker directs the attack from a standing position to an opponent in a seated posture.

3 **Suwari Waza** ... Both the attacker and defender begin in seated positions.

Techniques and movement beginning in seated posture are designed to make the practitioner more aware of using and strengthening the hips and lower body. It originates from the ancient times in Japanese culture when one may be attacked whilst in the home in a traditional seated posture. Therefore it was important to learn how to move and execute good technique from such a vulnerable start position. Once the ability is achieved where one may move easily from this posture then the value of the increase in power from the centre of the body is appreciated.

Shikko

Performing movements whilst in a seated position on both knees, one must learn the skill of walking on the knees. This knee walking is known as Shikko, it is also known as the Samurai Walk. It is incorporated in both method two and three.

Begin learning with method one, as shown in this book. It may soon be practised into the other methods when the time is appropriate.

The Basic Stance

Hanmi

Hanmi is the name given to the triangular stance used in all aspects of Aikido training, whether it be for basic tai jutsu movements or advanced weapons practice. This hanmi is designed to allow for rapid and easy movement in any direction.

To achieve correct Hidari hanmi (left stance):
1   Stand naturally, with both feet on a straight line.
2   Turn and look to your left. Allow your left foot to turn.
3   The left foot is now the front foot. The back foot may adjust slightly until it feels comfortable.
4   The body is distributed so that the leading leg is taking about two thirds of the weight.
5   Both knees are slightly bent.
6   The left hand is forward, with the fingers extended.
7   The right hand remains just above the waist. Keep both hands on the centre line of your body.
8   Migi hanmi (right stance) is the opposite of that shown. The right hand and right leg are forward.

The Centre Line

The centre line refers to the line that travels directly through the centre of the body, as shown in the diagram. When the body is in motion the hands will endeavour to retain a close relationship to this line. If both of the hands were by the sides of the body when an attack was launched at the face, the hands would have to travel a much further distance and hence would probably be too slow in defence.

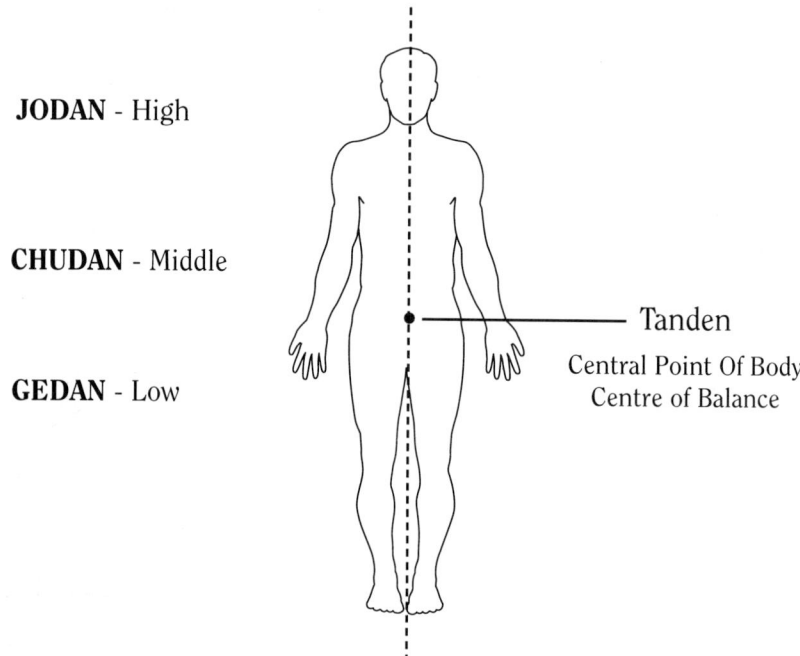

JODAN - High

CHUDAN - Middle

GEDAN - Low

Tanden
Central Point Of Body
Centre of Balance

Pivot - A method of turning on the balls of both feet, without lifting off the floor.

Training Exercise
Practise changing from left to right hanmi. Keeping both feet on the same line, turn from left to right, allowing the feet to turn naturally on the spot. The hands slide smoothly from side to side ALWAYS keeping above your own waist level. Do not drop this guard, it is your PROTECTION.

Left Hanmi
NORTH

turning

Right Hanmi
SOUTH

Tenkan and Tai Sabaki Movements

When the hanmi has been practised until it becomes a natural and comfortable posture, it is necessary to learn how to move in a correct manner. These two methods of movement are incorporated in many of Aikido techniques and allow the body freedom of movement.

Tenkan ..... From hanmi imagine that the front foot is nailed to the floor. It cannot step forward or backwards. A Tenkan movement is a pivot on the leading foot, so if the body is facing north, pivot on the front foot and take the back foot to the rear, so the body is now facing south. You are in the same hanmi but facing the opposite direction.

Shown below:
After the initial pivot on the left foot, take the right foot backwards in a straight line passing the left to assume hanmi.

Tenkan -----   180 degree pivot on the front foot.

NOTE The front hand (in the case of the photographs - left hand) and the front foot, turn INWARDS, to the centre of the body. This helps with the turning motion of the body as it begins to pivot.

KEEP THE HEAD UP. BE PROUD OF THE MOVEMENT.

Tai-Sabaki

From hanmi the rear foot takes a step forward travelling past the front foot. Now a Tenkan is made from this foot. To co-ordinate the body with the hand movements, it is important that when the initial step is taken, the rear hand travels forward to match it, acting as a guard on the centre line throughout.

In order to practise many repetitions correctly a few pointers are listed: Do NOT lift the feet up when in motion. It is far better to slide the soles of the feet along the floor, or matted area. This ensures that the body weight does not lift up and down during the movement, but this sliding action allows the body to move swiftly keeping the hips and therefore stability strong. Make a sliding sound as the feet travel. If there is no sound, then the feet are lifting too much off the floor.

Partnered Tai-Sabaki Practice

This is a partner practice that
(a) Develops good Tai-Sabaki, in relation to working with one's partner.
(b) Illustrates the importance of protecting the centre line.
(c) Encourages blending with the opponent and fluid body movements.

1 Stand in front of the partner. Both students to be in Ai-Hanmi with the front hand outstretched. The front hands make contact on the palms. Both students with the same leg forward.

2 To begin this exercise, one partner will complete the movement, whilst the other person remains stationary. As the Tai-Sabaki is initiated NOTE the back hand travels forward to guard the opponent's front hand.

3 Once one partner has completed the movement, it is time for the other person to make their Tai-Sabaki. It is important for them to make contact with the hands at the end of this motion, so the other person may begin again.

With practice, both students will be able to co-ordinate this movement without either one stopping or pausing. Simply by repetitive motion on both sides this becomes an excellent way to learn body-blending and fluidity of the body.

Now the other student executes his Tai-Sabaki movement, whilst the partner remains stationary.

Advanced levels:

As the speed of this movement increases it creates a fluid form. This is good, but it is important not to try and travel so fast that one's balance and basic posture deteriorate.

DO NOT SKIP TO GAIN SPEED. ALWAYS SLIDE.

Working with your Partner

From this point on your partner will be known as **Uke**. This is the Japanese term used for the attacker and hence the person who receives the technique. The student practising the techniques (the defender) will be known as **Nage**.

Maai is the correct distance between Nage and Uke. If two students are facing each other so that their noses are touching then the Maai is correct for one to head butt the other. However the Maai is incorrect for a punch to the face, the distance between them is far too close. Depending on the nature of the attack the Maai will adjust accordingly. In normal class practice the Maai is approximately an arm's length away from both Nage and Uke.

This shows Gyaku hanmi
Katatetori

Katatetori means
"One handed Seizure
from side"

Gyaku hanmi

Nage stands in left hanmi facing Uke. Uke assumes right hanmi. This means that Uke is in a reverse stance to Nage. If both students change their hanmi, they are still said to be in Gyaku hanmi (in relation to one another)

Katatetori - The leading wrist is firmly held by Uke.

The Katatetori Attack Explained

This form of learning is unique in many ways and is often associated with Aikido practice, as very few of the other martial art groups use this form. It is a method of learning and practising movement and techniques with one's partner, in a safe and sensitive way. One can directly feel the contact of the attacker upon one's wrist and how one's own movements and techniques react to the person holding. The feeling that one acquires through this form of practice is very important. Each attacker may hold with varying amounts of pressure which force the defender to react in a manner fit for that particular situation. At first, to the beginner, each movement and technique will be identical, going through the set patterns of motions and thought. This is a good educational form. Later on, once the student is fully aware of which particular action to apply, then the sensitive elements of reacting to the particular individual is applied. This is harmonising with the situation and will become a natural and instinctive way of thinking and reacting once attacked. Remember that each attack and attacker is unique, as is the corresponding defence. This is an advanced ideal and must not hinder the novice's thoughts of performing the set techniques that follow in this book. When one first learns to write it is very robotic and in copy-cat form, once acknowledged then one may feel how the pen moves performing the same tasks.

In the practice of the Katatetori form, it is important for Nage to extend the leading hand forward in order to 'Offer' the target area to be attacked. Naturally Uke will take hold of the nearest and therefore leading wrist. In the initial level one learns in Kihon, basic step by step form, as shown in this manual, which means that in this case Nage allows Uke to take the front wrist whilst it is a still target. Then once the take has been firmly made the Nage begins from this starting point.

Leading Uke

The next level of learning is the **Ki No Nagare** form. In order to utilise this, Nage now begins to 'Lead' the opponent. It must be noted that Nage must fully understand the basic body mechanics and correct positioning of both himself and Uke before attempting to lead Uke. Simply put, Nage desires to lead the attacking energy from Uke in a way that travels into the technique or movement that they wish to accomplish. Also Nage wishes to lead Uke's mind and intention. This is a much more advanced situation and will only be made clear through practice.

How to lead Uke using the Katatetori Form:
Nage stands in front of Uke with the leading arm and wrist extended, offering the desired target to be taken. Assume correct Maai. In advanced practice this Maai may be up to double that which has already been specified.

Uke steps forward to attempt to take the leading wrist. It is at this point that Nage leads Uke's forward momentum onward, creating a situation wherefore Uke is continually leaning forward to almost catch up to the arm/wrist which is being led away. Like the proverbial 'donkey and carrot' Uke must feel that he is almost about to reach the target but never actually gains a firm hold of it. Nage's timing is important to keep a little ahead of Uke in order to make him reach for the hand. This keeps the flow of force very continuous and fluid, as Nage easily re-directs it into the technique to be executed.

It is vital to note that if Nage is too quick or snatches the leading hand away too early, then Uke will not even try to reach it.

Think of someone asking you for a £5 note. As you reach into your pocket to grasp it, and take it out the person believes he is almost ready to receive it. You very naturally hold it up in sight of him and make out as if you are going to pass it over. As he reaches out to take it begin to slide it away. If done correctly he will automatically follow the movement to get the money. It is this subtle LEAD that creates motion and puts Nage in the immediate state of mind of taking control of the situation.

LEAD THE OPPONENT   CREATE MOMENTUM

TAKE CONTROL

Ai Hanmi

In this instance, Nage and Uke face each other in the same hanmi (both with either their left foot forward or their right foot forward). The picture below shows right hanmi, as if to shake hands.

To make Ai hanmi Katatetori:
Uke takes a firm hold of Nage's leading wrist. On both the defence and the attack, the leading leg (the front leg) is on the same side of the body as the hand being grabbed or the hand that is doing the taking.
This allows for Hanmi to be maintained.

Tai No Henko

This is a basic blending exercise initiated from a **Gyaku Hanmi Katatetori**. Its purpose is to obtain freedom of movement in a relaxed manner, even though the leading wrist is secured. When learning how to move, the grip is made slightly less dominant, so as not to hinder Nage's thoughts. When the movement is clear, the grip can be as strong as desired.

1 The picture shows Nage in left hanmi. Slide the leading foot towards the front foot of Uke's. Even though Nage's wrist is secured, his fingers can turn into the centre line as the leg advances. Advance the whole body forward in one motion.

2 From this foot perform a Tenkan.

3 Finish with both palms turned towards you. Both are equal.

NOTE The wrist stays where it is. Otherwise you are pulling or pushing your opponent. The aim is to move AROUND IT.

Gyaku Hanmi Katatetori Irimi-nage

Irimi-nage is a technique whereby Nage enters into Uke and employs a throw. **Irimi** means to enter, *nage* means to throw hence ... entering throw. So as not to cause confusion, the person known as Nage is therefore the thrower.

Assume the position shown on page 29, picture No. 2

1   Allow the back foot (left) to slide deeper in towards Uke. At the same time follow with the left hand up and across so that the forearm lifts Uke's chin. Extend the energy through your fingertips as the Uke's balance is broken.The right hand could also strike Uke's abdomen if desired. It should be noted that Nage's left elbow is positioned in line above Uke's Adam's apple, throat, in the case where it is needed to sharply strike downwards to finish.

2 Nage's whole body naturally slides forward, allowing both feet to continue in this direction. Nage's left arm extends which takes Uke to the floor. Practise slowly to allow your partner to gently fall to the floor.

3 As Uke falls away, turn the hips in time to make for good balance and correct hanmi.

BE EXPRESSIVE WITH THE FINGERS AND PALM

The aim is to give out energy, to and beyond your opponent.

Balance

Within Aikido movements, the opponent's balance must be disturbed or broken for the execution of a good throw or the application of technique. An opponent with good posture, remaining on balance, will be in a strong position to either resist the throw/technique or, more importantly, be able to continue with the assault.
There are several factors required to remain on firm balance:

Stance:
The legs must be adequately spaced to share the load of the body evenly. Try standing on one leg and see how much effort it takes for your partner to disturb your balance. It is considerably less than the effort required whilst both legs are firmly grounded. A stable base makes a stable top.

Head:
The head/brain controls the body. It is like a computer directing a machine, upset its function and the machine is affected. As a test close both eyes and take the head as though you were looking directly up to the sky, and then a little further back. It will be found that one's sense of balance is unsure. It should be noted that whilst performing the Irimi nage technique Uke's head goes through this position.
If one were to combine these two factors then standing on one leg and taking the head backwards would result in a reduction or loss of stability (as a strike to the face)
It can be seen that it is vital to maintain a strong body and head posture throughout the execution of movement. Knowing this information is important so that, whilst performing the movements and techniques, one bears in mind one's own body and head posture is strong and stable.

It is important to understand the methods used in Aikido that upset or break the opponent's balance sufficiently to continue further with the required actions. Whilst there are many different methods of "balance disturbance", some using a combination, it will be easier to understand these methods when separated and explained into their individual parts. The three areas used for the disturbance of balance are listed:

1 STRIKE / BLOW
The most primitive way of affecting the opponent's balance is by means of a physical strike. A punch to the jaw, or a sharp jab to the solar plexus

(under the sternum), or a direct kick to the shinbone will result in a momentarily loss of balance. Although Aikido is not designed to destroy the aggressor outright by means of one strike, it is important to acknowledge the fact that in some instances a correctly delivered strike will be an option worth future consideration. There may not be enough time or perhaps enough room to perform much movement of technique. In these situations the knowledge of "striking" is useful. In martial arts the most generally accepted striking weapon is the closed fist. In Aikido however, one does not train specifically on developing the focus and strength needed when the fist makes impact on its target. For persons who do not wish to train for impact/conditioning of their wrist, knuckles etc. then other methods of striking must be considered. These are listed below:

The Edge of the Hand:
The line running from the tip of the little finger underside to the base of the wrist. To be used in a chopping downwards or sidewards motion.

The Heel (palm) of the Hand:
The base of the palm, where the inner thumb muscle is located. Rather than using a fist to the face or jaw this method of contact is very powerful. One could quite easily make a firm impact to a solid wall, without any prior conditioning and resulting in no injury to the hand. One could not strike a solid wall with a closed fist in the same manner. A very good striking utility.

The Fingers:
To be used for scratching, poking and even for pinching. Imagine one's opponent has you in a firm strangle hold, with both their hands firmly squeezing the throat. In little time one cannot breathe and becomes a victim. Position one's two hands underneath the upper arms of the attacker, on the triceps. Apply a tight, sharp pinch to the lower triceps. This will result in severe pain causing a release of the strangle grip. At this point once the attacker has lost his intention one may apply technique. This is referred to as **Atemi Waza**

Atemi Waza
This is the use of skilful striking in order to proceed with technique. As Aikido is not designed to retaliate force with force then the difference between using Atemi rather than using a counter-strike method must be

understood. The difference is that one uses an Atemi in order to be able to proceed further with a desired technique or movement. It is used as a DISTRACTION. It could be considered a back up plan so one may achieve the desired goal of executing good, pure Aikido.

A few examples and reasons of why Atemi may be used are listed below:

1 **Distraction**

Imagine once more that the opponent has both hands tightened around one's throat. A short sharp flick with the ends of the fingers to the attacker's eyes will be enough to distract him whilst one applies technique. A flick like this, especially if with sharp fingernails, can be as effective as a punch, but the amount of effort needed for its execution is a great deal less.

2 **Control of Speed**

If the attacker is approaching with too much speed then a correctly delivered strike will alter this speed to the required level for a technique to follow. This is a basic method. This theory also works the opposite way in that by applying a strike to a static attack this will create movement to be utilised in technique or a throw.

3 **Maai**

To maintain the correct distance. An opponent seeing a strike coming towards him will naturally either slow down or retreat.

It is important that an Atemi is used only when it is needed. If it is used as a finishing blow then the ideals of Aikido are not being employed. Be aware that once the strike is made it will make the assailant react in some way. It is of little benefit executing a strike that makes the opponent travel backwards when one wishes to apply a technique which requires the opponent to have a forward loss of balance.

ACTION EQUALS REACTION

Be knowledgeable as to how the opponent will react after receiving the impact, or intention.

2 PERPENDICULAR THEORY

The way in which one stands, i.e. stance, is of vital significance in maintaining good balance of the upper body. The perpendicular theory is a basis by which one can determine the weakest angle of a person's stance in order to utilise it during technique. This angle is a right angle.

Ask your partner to stand in a strong / solid stance. In reality this means very little as a person's stance will only be strong in relation to the line of effort that is exerted upon it. This will become clear with this experiment.

Assume one's partner has the right foot forward in a wide hanmi posture. If one were to stand directly in front of him and push towards him then he would be able to resist a significant amount of this force. This push could be channelled through his rear leg / foot as this foot would be able to act as an anchor in retaliation.

Keeping your partner in the same stance, draw a straight line from the big toe of the front foot to the big toe of the rear foot. In the middle of this line draw another line at a right angle to it. If one positions oneself on this line only a small amount of effort is required to destroy the balance of the opponent. It should be observed that by the correct positioning of oneself in the relationship to one's attacker this same angle is utilised (even though only momentarily) in many cases. Within the basic techniques of Aikido the appropriate angles have already been incorporated to provide all the possible advantages over one's adversary.

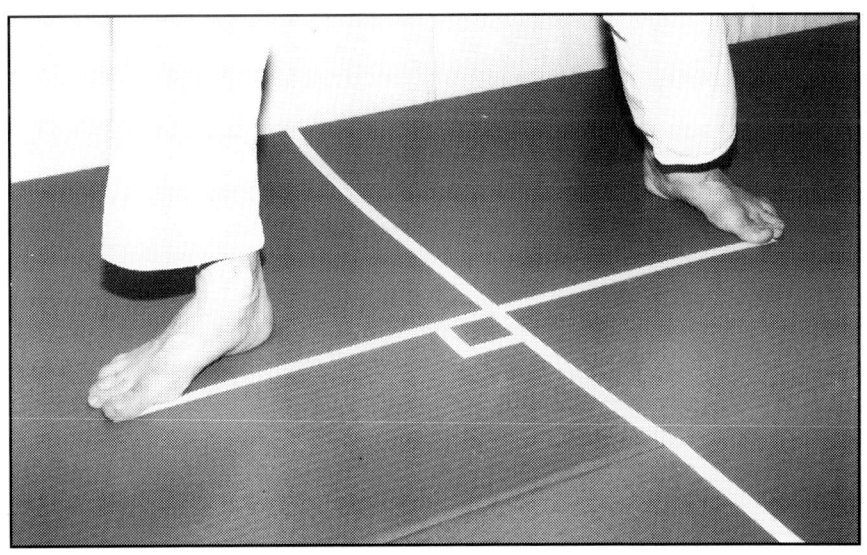

MOTION -FLUIDITY

This is a more advanced method of taking control of the partner's balance. It is done by utilising timing and extension. This will become more relative as one's knowledge and practice experience is increased. However as a simple guide it could be explained as follows:

Imagine stretching out your hand to push open a door - a door that opens away from you. Just at the point where you are about to exert effort to push the door open, someone else opens the door from the other side. Momentarily you are outstretched and have lost your balance. This same concept is applied when an attacker is lunging forward to push you back. If you can time it correctly and take the motion in the same direction, the attacker will be over extended and the balance broken. Adapting this method, the technique will flow and the Uke will appear to be very light and easy to manipulate into the appropriate motions.

Once we are able to position ourselves in respect to Uke during practice, and in respect to people with whom we come into contact throughout our daily lives, in the correct position that enables our own balance to be strong and theirs not so strong, then we gain an advantageous position, whether it be for business or for personal reasons.
e.g. A top business man would prefer to sit behind a big desk on a chair that allows him to be in a higher position than an interviewee sitting opposite.

POSITIONING ADVANTAGES

Irimi-nage from a Punch (Tsuki)

The principle of the technique is the same as the form which has previously been shown with the Katatetori attack. However, as Black Star's first objective is to protect oneself, naturally one must be out of the way of the punch before the technique is employed.

1 Both partners begin on the same line. As the punch travels to its target (in this case the stomach) Nage must move off line. In order to guarantee that it misses, the leading hand covers the body as it moves across.

The leading hand does NOT block the punch, it simply acts as a guard as the whole body moves off line.

2   The position of Nage's body is now sliding forward, whilst the hands are constantly moving. As in the picture Nage's back (right) hand takes control of the punch and allows it to carry on in the same direction.

3   This stretches Uke and with the two hands working together, breaks his balance. One has the feeling of keeping Uke's arms fully stretched throughout the motion, as if using a bow & arrow, gradually but continuously working until the end.

INITIAL DEFENCE

The defending hand is very important in the way it positions itself upon Uke's attacking punch/wrist/forearm. It does not grab or take the oncoming strike, only deflect and protect. Note this hand's edge is used. The blade of the hand running from the top of the little finger to the base of wrist is in contact. Also, this arm's elbow is low, thus allowing more cover and protection to the body.

Gyaku hanmi Katatetori Nikkyo

Nikkyo is a wrist technique in which pressure is applied on the wrist, causing the attacker great discomfort and resulting in a submission or the body to be immobilised.

1 Nage is in a dangerous position by being on the same line as Uke. The initial step to the side (in the case of the photo below) is done by moving the left foot off-line and forward. The back foot must advance so as to keep on good posture. Nage's left hand points across, so Uke's leading arm is stretched causing him to be weak. It is important that Nage's free hand remains on the centre line and is, also extended to maintain the correct Maai, so you are out of reach of the attacker's opposite hand.

2 Nage's right hand takes the back of Uke's attacking hand and places it on the chest, keeping it well turned over at all times.

3 Nage's left hand and elbow act upon Uke's arm in a turning motion. As shown, Nage's right hand is turning in the opposite direction. **Nage must create a small bend in Uke's arm**. The balance between the turning motion and the downward motion of Nage's arms must be PRACTISED.

4 It is important to be aware of Uke's free hand, and its reach. If it is too close to you whilst applying the Nikkyo, then simply adjust the Maai so it is safe to continue. In real terms this free hand may conceal a knife, so stay away from it. This awareness in mind and body greatly enhances the defence capabilities and everyday well being.

Nikkyo from a Punch (Tsuki)

The technique is executed in the same manner as already described with the Katatetori form. Once the attack has been dealt with, the Nikkyo can be performed.

1 Both partners begin on the same line. Uke steps forward with the back foot whilst lunging a punch towards Nage. For safety reasons during practice the punch is aimed for the chest area. However, this opening sequence may easily be adapted to a punch to the jaw.

2 Nage steps off line. The front foot slides to the side first with the rear foot following to maintain balance and hanmi. The leading hand and forearm guards the body as it moves off line.

3 Nage's leading hand guides over the top of Uke's attacking arm and circles downwards and to the side. The energy of the fist is dispersed with this motion. To keep good Maai, note that Nage has altered his body alignment to Uke, this extra space allows for the safe position in which to apply the Nikkyo.

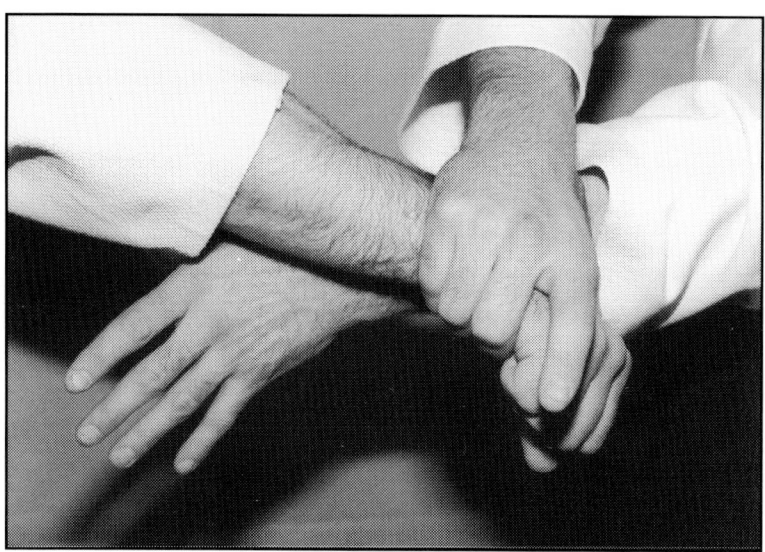

4 Nage's right hand takes control of the punching fist, being firmly gripped on the back of the fist. Both Nage's hands are raised so that the locked fist may be placed on Nage's chest, as with the basic form. APPLY NIKKYO.

Katatori Nikkyo

Katatori is the name for the attack whereby Nage's lapel or shoulder is taken. This attack on its own is relatively harmless, but it must be considered in most cases that this pinning or holding is undertaken for the purpose of keeping the target still whilst it is struck.

1   Both students assume Gyaku hanmi. Uke takes a good hold of Nage's clothing. The first principle of movement must be made, and that is to step off the same line as Uke. It can be clearly seen that if one remains on the same line (directly in front of the attacker) then one is easily targeted by Uke's free hand.

2   Nage's front foot slides to the outside and across, so that Uke's attacking arm is stretched. At the same time Nage's free hand (in this case the right hand) travels in front of Uke's face and then down to assume the basic Nikkyo form.

3 Whilst executing the distraction to Uke's face, the rear foot must slide across also to make for a good balance and correct hanmi.

4 Notice the rear foot has travelled even further around so Nage is in a good position to complete the Nikkyo technique as in the previous methods.

IMPORTANT

If Uke takes a really secure hold of the material and keeps it tight within the grip, then performs the turning of this wrist in the shoulder area, turning the shoulder inwards will help to turn Uke's wrist encased in the jacket.

Ryotetori Tenchi Nage

Ryotetori is the name of an attack whereby both Nage's hands are taken from the front. It is a very beneficial way of practising as both hands and therefore both sides of the body must work in co-ordination with one another. It encourages the whole of the body to operate as one unit. An arm on its own has little strength in comparison to its power when backed up with the power of the whole body.

Tenchi Nage means heaven and earth throw. One hand points to heaven whilst the other points to earth (as in photo 2).

1   Both Nage's wrists are taken, Nage is in left Hanmi. Uke assumes gyaku hanmi in relation to Nage (in this case Uke has his right foot forward).

2   Nage slides his leading foot to the outside of Uke's body (this slide forces Uke's posture to become weaker). At the same time the front foot slides over, the hand points across and down, stretching Uke's arm and breaking his balance.

3 Nage's other hand is working all the time but is pointing up and through Uke's elbow. Nage must make sure that he does not lift his elbow up whilst performing this move, as it will allow Uke to resist the actions of this upward movement.

4 As Nage steps forward and through with the back foot, the right hand turns in a circular motion around Uke's shoulder area and finishes pointing towards the ground. Both arms are extended. Finish in good posture, otherwise Uke will drag you down with him as he falls away from you in order to protect himself.

The Expression of the Hands - Ryotetori Tenchi Nage

Aikido is not merely a way of disarming and adversary or inflicting painful techniques on your opponents, but also a way in which to express oneself. The hands are a simple means of showing outward signs of how we feel. Some people use their hands very expressively whilst talking, it is a means of exaggerating a point. In this case, a means to allow energy to flow out of Nage in the right directions.

The way in which the hands are used is a good focal point whilst training. Think of energising a sphere in the palms of your hands, and then later on in practice one will be able to achieve the sensation of throwing the energised spheres away. Aikido deals with understanding energy, whether it be the energy used by your opponent in a savage attack, or the energy used in everyday life. In both cases, learning how to accept and use these different energies in the most natural way possible will lead to a better understanding of those around you and most importantly of all........ the understanding of the SELF.

Ryokatatori Tenchi-Nage

Tenchi Nage from a two handed jacket grab

In order to apply Tenchi Nage from an opponent attempting to take a firm hold of one's jacket, it is important that Nage reacts spontaneously with the oncoming attack. If Nage remains static, then the attacker will have an easy task of pinning the victim to the spot by holding his jacket. This occurs when the Maai is broken. Nage must be in control of the Maai and therefore will not be in this predicament.

As Uke attempts to take hold of the jacket, Nage intercepts the motion by bringing his two hands up and inside the opponent's. Keep both thumbs in tight to avoid breaking them. As with the basic form of Tenchi Nage, Nage guides Uke's arms so taking them off posture, whilst the top hand is preparing to continue with the Tenchi Nage.

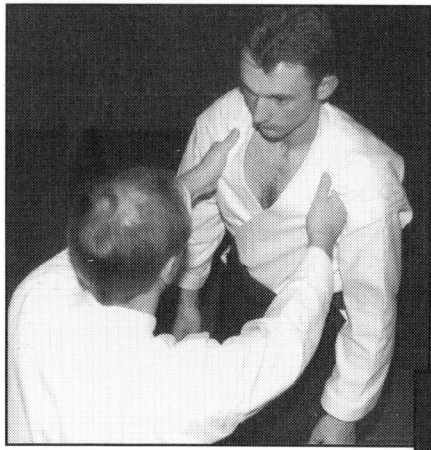

1

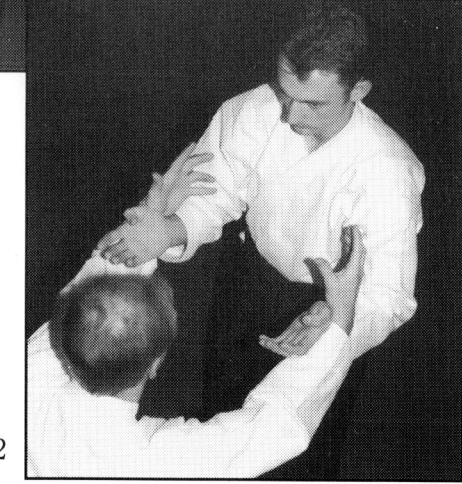

2

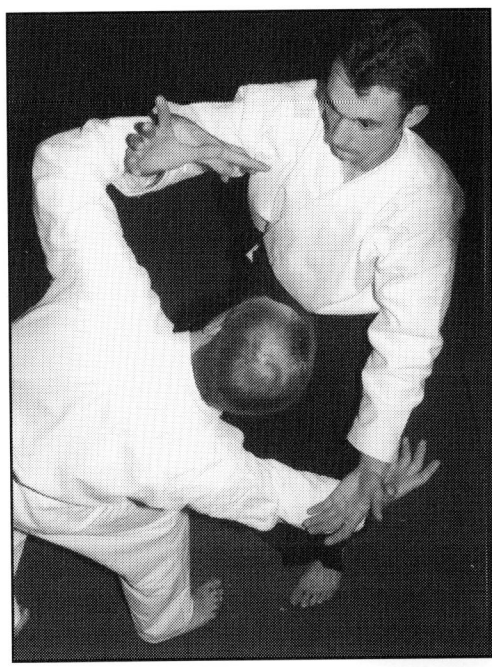

3

4

If Uke is moving in with speed to grab the jacket, then Nage MUST slide back accordingly as the attacking motion becomes closer, at the same time using the two hands. Nage moves back in the same hanmi. Do not step back, just slide the whole body back as necessary.

Nage takes control of Uke's lower wrist, to guide him off posture. As the balance is broken, Nage moves in to finish the technique.

5

Be sure to keep Uke's balance broken whilst stepping in and through. This is maintained by keeping the lower arm outstretched.

SAFETY .... Remember Uke is falling to the floor, so allow him to fall at his own speed (whilst learning), this will enable Uke to fall naturally, without hurting himself. The art of falling correctly is called Practising Ukemi, hence the term Uke. Ukemi applies to all rolling and breakfalling of Uke.

Nage and Uke learn together, so take care of your training partner, and the progress of both students will accumulate. After sustained regular practice Nage will understand that a partner who attacks and falls well is a much better training person to work with. Uke acts almost as a mirror, reflecting truly, the techniques and movements that Nage is trying upon them. A good Uke will be a good mirror, enabling Nage to see any mistakes that need correcting. The trust that grows between the two persons will allow for ease and relaxed motions to be carried out. All Aikido should be practised with a relaxed but alert mind, with non mental aggression towards one's attacker. This allows one to be void to the attacker's negative thoughts and therefore actions. Lead one's attacker to reach your positive state, do not let them lead you into their negative state. Naturally a good, positive Uke, and Nage rub off on each other, thus increasing progression.

Morotetori Ikkyo

Morotetori is the name for the attack whereby Uke takes a grip of Nage's forearm with both hands.

Ikkyo is an immobilization technique. Ikkyo uses the control of Uke's elbow and wrist to manipulate the body into becoming unbalanced and finally pinned to the floor.

1 Uke grabs Nage's forearm with both hands. The front leg of Uke is the same side forward as the top hand doing the taking. Both are in Gyaku hanmi to one another. Note how easy it is to punch Uke's face, as his two hands are tied up holding you. Learn the motion before applying extra parts to the whole.

2 Slide the front foot forward and to the side of Uke, the rear foot makes hanmi. Nage drops the elbow of the arm that is being seized. It must be understood that Nage can move the elbow because it is not being held, (the forearm is held). Once the elbow is low then Nage may circle the hand upwards and outwards. To allow the energy from the hand to flow out keep the fingers open and slightly stretched (focused).

3 To bring Uke off posture, Nage takes the rear foot to make hanmi in a position perpendicular to Uke. i.e. at right angles to him.

The Correct Feeling and Tension
Look at Uke's grip. If Nage's wrist/forearm is very rigid then Uke will be able to hold and squeeze upon it much more easily, resulting in Nage's initial movements to be made more limited. Nage must relax the arm being seized. A simple rule that applies: It is easy to apply a strong grip onto something solid, e.g a housebrick, but try and grip a sponge (Note the likeness to Nage's relaxed arm) it becomes less instinctive. One cannot receive the same feedback from a soft item, in order to exert more effort in the grip.

NAGE: RELAXED BUT FOCUSED IS THE KEY.

4 Nage takes the front foot directly back in a straight line. This will bring Uke forward and around. Nage's leading arm travels in a circular motion in order to expose Uke's elbow and takes a firm position on Uke's elbow with the free hand (left). This is the control.

5 Nage brings both the arms down whilst sliding in towards Uke.

6 Stepping in deep and extending Uke's arm through their opposite shoulder, Uke will have no balance.

7 When Uke is on the floor, the knee relating to the same side of Nage's body that is controlling the elbow, kneels down first. The other knee at this point remains off the floor.

8 The other knee slides down to the floor as the arm of Uke is lowered to its final position.

This is the final position to be assumed from all Ikkyo techniques.

Ikkyo Finishing Posture

The photograph shows the link between the central point of the Black Star logo to the use of the central point of Nage.

Whilst it can be easily understood that the energy is emitted from the central point in both cases, and travelling outwards through the arms into the fingertips, in the case of the Ikkyo Pin, to master this feeling will take much practice and serious study.

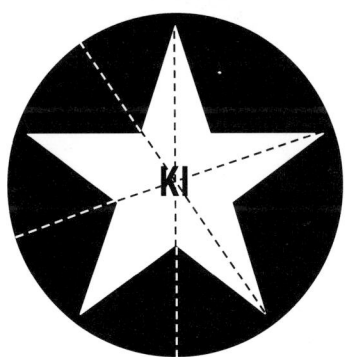

Note...The fingers of each hand are pointing towards one another so that the energy is easily circled, fed around in a continuous motion.

Energised Spheres: If one turns back to the concept of energising the spheres in the palms of the hands and now understands that this energy is itself a larger sphere located/stored at the central point of oneself, yet again a new understanding will prevail.

Ai-hanmi Katatetori Ikkyo

Uke takes Nage's leading wrist, in Ai hanmi form. Nage and Uke are on the same line. Nage's leading hand is palm down.

Nage steps to the side and forward with the leading foot. The rear foot begins to slide forward in order that Nage may keep on good balance. As Nage's body is advancing, the front hand rises. Extend the fingers and push against Uke's wrist with the blade of the hand (the edge running from the tip of the little finger and down to the base of the wrist). Do not grip Uke's wrist with this hand, but concentrate on extending energy through the fingers and arms. This creates a small bend in Uke's arm, with Uke's elbow raised high.

Nage's rear hand takes up the position on the elbow of Uke's raised arm, as in Morotetori Ikkyo. Extend this arm. Nage's hips turn as both the arms circle downwards to the mat. Both Nage's arms are extended. If Nage feels too far away at any point from Uke during the movement then it is quite acceptable for them to slide in closer with the feet. This keeps for an adjustable Maai situation, Nage learns to move in order to keep the Maai to a distance most suitable for the particular technique.

Nage takes Uke down to the floor. Ikkyo finish. The hands stay in this position until Nage walks away.

Ai-hanmi Katatetori Kotegaeshi

Kotegaeshi is a wrist technique in which pressure is applied on the wrist away from Uke's body, the result being that Uke is taken to the floor in either a straight down motion or by a more advanced means where Uke is thrown down and away. The basic way is shown:

1 Nage and Uke are in Ai-hanmi. The picture shows Right hanmi. Uke takes Nage's leading wrist (right). Nage's palm of the leading hand faces up towards the ceiling.

2 Nage turns this palm in a circular motion to face Uke, (as if waving to say goodbye). This action exposes Uke's inner forearm, as circled.

3 Nage's back foot (left) steps in to the outside of Uke's front foot. At the same time, the left hand travels forward to take on top of Uke's exposed inner forearm. Nage turns and faces to the rear, the same way as Uke is facing. Naturally the hanmi adjusts when the hips turn.

4 Nage's right foot takes a position perpendicular to Uke's front foot. Both hands draw Uke's arm so that Uke is off balance. Uke should almost be falling on top of you. In order for Uke to correct his balance a step forward is taken with the back foot.

5 As Uke is falling towards Nage, Nage slides the front foot (left) back. This allows a space for Uke to continue to fall and therefore be off balance and weak.

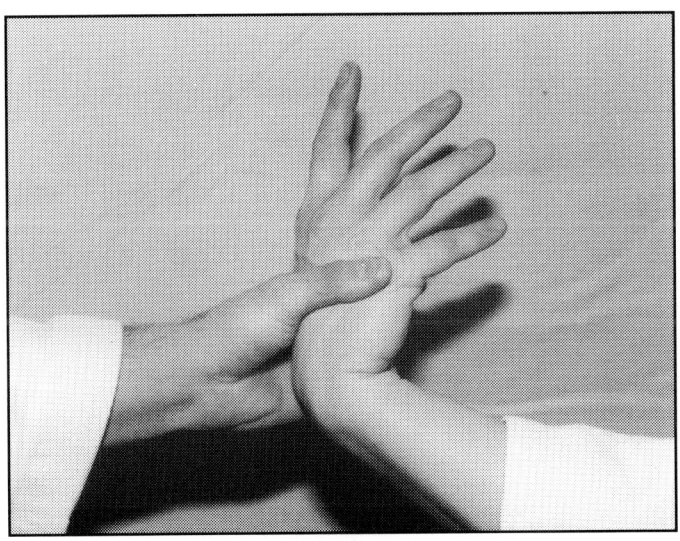

6 Nage peels the right hand out of Uke's grip, if it has not already broken away, due to the movement. Nage's left hand takes a position on the back of Uke's wrist whereby Nage's thumb is pushing through Uke's little finger knuckle.

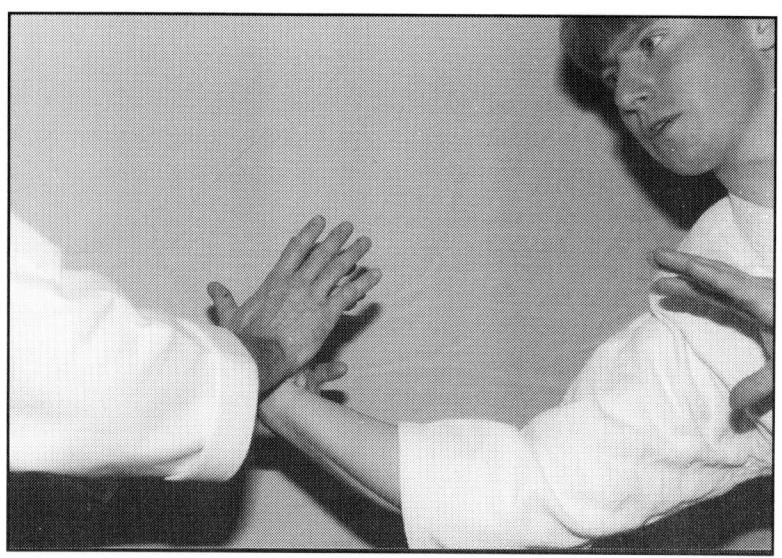

7   Nage's right hand is placed on the edge of the wrist in progress.
    Nage's two hands turn and circle down to the floor. This turning
    motion on Uke's wrist is painful and results in Uke going down to the
    floor to escape the pain.

8   As Uke falls, Nage must turn the hips and hanmi so that a good
    finishing posture is achieved.

Shomenuchi - The Attack

Aikido as a martial art must be able to deal with all kinds of different attacks. Up to this point one has learnt how to deal with being grabbed and punched in different situations.

Shomen translates as the centre of the head. **Uchi** is the word for a strike, therefore **Shomenuchi** is a strike to the centre of the head.

How to perform the Attack:
1   Uke attacks the centre of Nage's head with the hand blade. To amplify the attack Uke steps forward with the back foot and delivers the strike with the same hand forward. The two students are in Ai-hanmi as the blow meets its target.

IMPORTANT... when the other hand of Uke is used to deliver the strike, then Nage stands in opposite hanmi. This makes for Ai-hanmi form to be kept.

In reality the strike represents being struck with an object whether it be a baseball bat or a broken bottle, so treat the attack seriously.

Shomenuchi Kotegaeshi

The basic technique of Kotegaeshi is applied. The only difference now is the attack. Once the attack has been dealt with, the basic form of Kotegaeshi is carried out.

REMEMBER: Keep to the First Objective.... self-defence.

Both Nage and Uke start in Gyaku hanmi, so that when Uke steps forward with the back foot and strikes with the back hand Ai-hanmi form is made. Nage keeps the hands low in order to entice Uke into making a head strike.

As Uke's strike is coming down and Uke has stepped forward Nage raises the front hand high in order to begin guiding its power.

As the strike travels down, Nage steps off the attacking line. The front foot moves across first, followed naturally by the rear foot in order to make hanmi. Nage's leading arm lets the attack slip by, acting as a protective insurance. The arm is not acting as a block. The whole body has moved.

As the initial part of this technique is so important (in real terms if one cannot accomplish this part correctly then one is hit and cannot carry on) it is advised that the students practise this part many times until a confident attitude and movement is attained.

1. Nage's front hand guides the power of Uke's strike down and slightly extended away. Nage begins to turn the hips to face Uke. Nage's attention is towards the attacker, NOT the attacking limb.

2. Nage's back foot (left) and back hand (left) travel forward. The back foot positions itself in line with Uke's front foot, and to the outside. The back hand assumes the basic position on the top of Uke's wrist, as is for Ai hanmi Kotegaeshi. Nage turns to face the same direction as Uke. The hanmi changes accordingly.

3. Uke continues to fall forward as the momentum of his attack is extended forward. With increased speed and utilisation of Uke's attacking force, Nage may make a variable Tai Sabaki to absorb the power initially. This will be clearer through practice. Now practise 1 to 3 so that they become one movement. As the hips and whole body turn from 2 to 3 Nage should feel very positive and energised.

4 Nage's right foot takes a position at right angles to Uke's feet (as with basic). Note that in order to keep Uke off balance and his arm outstretched, Nage has also slid back the front foot. Correct Maai is assumed.

5. Apply Kotegaeshi. Turn hips and make for a good finish.

Ai hanmi Katatetori Shihonage

Shihonage is a technique in which pressure is applied against Uke's wrist and elbow, utilising a sword swinging motion to throw Uke down. Shihonage is a four-directional throw. The most common direction is shown:

1 Assuming Ai hanmi Uke takes Nage's wrist, Nage's hand is palm up.

2 With the thumb outstretched on the leading hand, Nage circles it over the top of Uke's wrist. At the same time the front foot slides forward and to the side. Nage takes Uke's arm out to the side, beginning to break his balance. Whilst at this point of the technique note that Uke's free hand and corresponding shoulder should be turned away, so that it cannot reach you. If Uke can touch you with his free hand then he is not sufficiently off posture/balance, so step a little further away to create enough space and the necessary angle.

3 Nage's rear hand is placed alongside the other. Both Nage's thumbs are in position, one points up and the other points down (AS SHOWN 3a).

(3a)

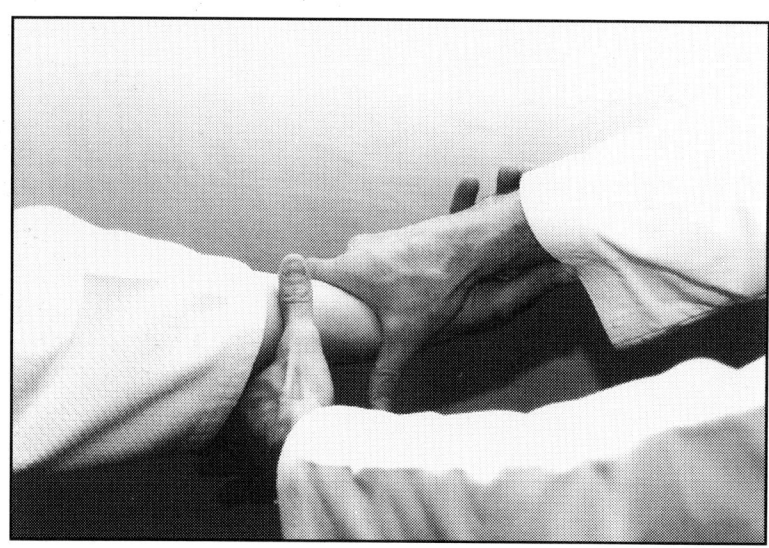

4 Nage keeps the two arms at length and steps forward and in with the rear foot. In the case of the side shown, Nage's left elbow is pushing against Uke's elbow. As Nage's elbow pushes up, the right hand remains low for a short time. This means that there is pressure against Uke's arm, as it is being levered. On a very primitive level, the arm could quite easily be broken at this point, however we do not wish for that amount of tension.

5 Taking the two hands over the head, Nage starts to turn on the balls of both feet to face the opposite direction, north to south. It can be seen how the turning exercise on the balls of both feet practised earlier lends itself to this technique.

6 Nage's hanmi is now facing the opposite direction, with Uke's elbow high, the take down is easily done. It is this turning and taking down that relates to the sword swinging motion. This will become evident in the uses of the Bokken.

7 As Uke falls away from Nage, in order that Nage remains on balance, Nage slides the feet and body forward to make for a solid finishing posture.

Nage takes both hands down to the floor, but the left hand is put to the centre line after Uke is motionless on the ground. This allows Nage to be in a more stable position.

Yokomenuchi - The Attack

Yokomen translates as the side of the head, therefore Yokomenuchi is an attack to the side of the head. In reality this attack may be a slashing type of attack with a knife or a crack to the side of the head with a broken bottle. By learning Yokomenuchi in a traditional format these aspects are covered.

How to perform the attack:
As with the Shomenuchi attack, Uke launches the strike from the back hand, stepping forward with the back foot.
NOTE... when Uke's handblade meets its target, Gyaku hanmi is formed between Uke and Nage. This is the formal way. Uke raises the back hand and takes it over the top of his head. As the rear foot travels forward, the attacking hand comes down at a slight angle to meet the side of Nage's head.
The strike meets its target. In practice it is very important that the attack is aimed and delivered properly. If Nage learns the defences from an attack that is not focused on a specific target then Nage is being cheated by Uke. If Uke is to make Yokomenuchi or Shomenuchi then that is exactly what should be done. He must not be lazy and just wave his arm up and down to look like the attack.

To Uke;
Concentrate on a positive, focused strike. It does NOT need to be fast or executed with too much power. This may be incorporated later when Nage has developed good foundations.

Yokomenuchi Shihonage

As with the basic Ai hanmi Shihonage (Katatetori) form the only alteration to be made is to deal with the attacking force and blend it into the technique to be done. In practice it can be experienced how easily the attacking Yokomenuchi can be led into the Shihonage.

NOTE The principle of using the aggressor's power against himself is adopted here. The harder they hit you the harder they fall - feeding energy into technique and movement.

1 Assuming Ai hanmi postures, Uke attacks Yokomenuchi from the back hand and back foot stepping in. This keeps the strike landing in Gyaku hanmi, to Nage.

2   Nage's leading arm raises up to guard against the oncoming blow. In time with the blow missing its target, Nage's back foot steps forward and across so it is on the same line as the front foot. This is only a temporary position so hanmi is not formed at this point. Remember the raised hand is NOT blocking the strike, it is merely guarding the head as the body is moving off line to execute the technique.

3 As the raised hand of Nage guides the striking arm of Uke down, Nage's original front foot (in this case .. left) becomes the back foot, making hanmi in this position. Doing this with the feet allows a space for the attacking force (arm) to be taken. The power of the blow is absorbed in this space. Nage feeds Uke's attacking wrist into his right open hand which is waiting to take control of it. Turn the hips and place the hands in the ready position to perform Shihonage. It is important to note that Nage's right hand (in this case) keeps protection of the centre line and does not eagerly cross over to grab Uke's attacking arm, thus no protection on the centre line. Perform Shihonage as already practised.

TRY AND FEEL THE POWER OF THE STRIKE BEING FED INTO YOUR TECHNIQUE... THEN YOU ARE USING THEIR ENERGY FOR YOUR BENEFIT.

Aikido Weaponry

During the study of Aikido, the practice of its associated weaponry, the Jo and Bokken are very important. Each weapon is used as a training aid to enhance the specific skills and knowledge needed for the performance of good Aikido.

The relationships that exist between the use of the weapons and the use of the the empty hands will soon become clear. This relationship is fundamentally Aikido. A way of blending regular practice with the Jo and Bokken will not only make for interesting and varied training sessions but will help assist the tai jutsu with the development of:

Creating a good base (Basing one's centre). A strong plateau from which to execute good techniques / maintain a firm finish.

Good posture (hanmi)

Positive and co-ordinated hand movements

Correct body positioning within technique

Focus and the use of Maai

Controlled breathing

Confident attitude and self discipline

Extension of Power (energy, ki)

A strong grip

The use of the weapons encourages a habit of maintaining the hands on the centre line.

TAI JUTSU + BOKKEN + JO = AIKIDO
By understanding each part, we can understand the whole.

The following sections explain how each weapon is used and the basic learning exercises are given. An outline of the way in which one may continue further with each weapon is given so that if one wishes to take levels of learning higher one has a direction in which to follow.

Bokken

Cutting through the Conflict
The Blade runs true

The Bokken

In appearance the **Bokken** is the wooden equivalent of the traditional Samurai Katana (forged sword). It is usually made from either red or white oak and is used in some martial arts as a safe way of learning swordsmanship. However the Bokken can be considered as a weapon in its own right as it has been proved combat efficient by Japanese feudal warriors.

The student of Aikido learns how to use the Bokken for the beneficial results it can provide. This practice is referred to as Aiki ken. There is little attention to the use of the live bladed sword, as this is another discipline known as Iaido, "the way of the sword"

The basic stages of learning the Bokken are:

1 **Bokken Suburi** - Singular exercise performed alone. One movement practised with focus and extension of Ki. Beginning the understanding of how to use the weapon. Also known as Ken Suburi, (a shortened term). Ken means sword.

2 **Tachi Dori** - Techniques of taking an opponent's sword and throwing him. Tachi is another term for Japanese sword. Tachi Dori - Sword taking.

Once the Bokken can be used competently, an advanced form of partner practice may be done with both students using a Bokken.

3 **Kumi tachi** - Advanced Bokken practice done with a partner. Blending practice of movements performed through attack and defence. Each partner performs a pre-arranged sequence. Through this type of practice one learns to move correctly under the continuous motion of defending and attacking, being able to move from one pattern into another. Natural actions and the flow of the body, both vital for Aikido.

How to hold the Bokken:

1   The Bokken is ALWAYS held in right hanmi. Naturally the right foot and hand are forward, with the left hand taking a firm position on the very end of the handle. There is a space between the two hands, depending on personal preference and the requirement dictated by the weight of the particular Bokken. Both hands are on the centre line.
The start position: the tip of the Bokken points towards an imaginary opponent's throat.

When using the Bokken, keep a firm grip with the little fingers first, then the other fingers wrapping around until a secure hold is achieved. NOTE the thumbs do not bear any tension in this grip.

For safety reasons it is recommended that the tip of the Bokken is sawn off to make it blunt. Most weapons are manufactured with a sharp point at the tip, so it is advisable for Aikido practice to remove it.

Keep the shoulders relaxed and down. Both arms are very slightly bent.

Once the Bokken is held so it feels comfortable, it is time to start learning how to operate it with the motion of the body.

Bokken Suburi

Suburi is a solo exercise performed with the Jo or Bokken. As it is performed alone, there is no excuse for the lack or neglect of practice. Whilst training, pay particular attention to correct form (movement), there is no need to execute the suburi with a great deal of physical strength. It is an education first, not a workout.

Cutting with the Bokken
The term used for making a downward strike.
Assume right hanmi. Take the Bokken in a vertical line over the head, continuing down the spine. To allow the body to become involved, the front foot slides smoothly back as the hands raise the Bokken. This foot only travels a little back and does not go past the rear foot (left).
As the Bokken travels forward to make the cut, the front foot follows.

N.B. Breathe in as the Bokken is raised. Inhale through the nose. Breathe out as the Bokken is cutting. Exhale through the mouth. Do not exhale all of the breath. When the body is emptied of all its natural air, it will feel weak, so hold a little in. This will be made clear through repetition.

The finishing posture should feel strong and well balanced.
The Bokken is parallel to the ground.

Education for Correct Breathing:
The practice of all movement within Aikido requires one to breathe, as does living. One must breathe to stay alive. Breathing correctly is important. Up till now the breath cycle during techniques has not been specified. This is because the student has been left to breathe naturally without thinking. Aikido is natural, so should be the breathing cycle involved. The weapons training in particular amplifies one's breathing to make sure it is positive and correct. A simple exercise to show how it feels when one breathes incorrectly is as follows: Lie down flat on the ground. Stand up and breathe OUT heavily. One will find it makes getting up very hard and tiring. Now do it right and breathe in on the effort, the standing up - It is now natural and easy.

Cutting with The Bokken

This basic movement is known as 'Bokken Suburi One'.

The hands and arms

As much repetition of cutting practice with the Jo and Bokken alike will take place, it is important to make sure that the hands and arms work in a correct manner so that good habits will form. The manner in which the arms work, both in the upward and downward cutting movement with the weapons, is the same way that is applied to empty handed training. Techniques previously practised, such as **Ikkyo**, in relation to the initial upward motion of the leading arm, and **Shihonage**, in the downward cutting motion, are the same. It can be seen how this training enhances the focus and co-ordination of the arms when performing basic technique with one's partner.

The left hand on the Bokken is responsible for bringing the power down, whilst the right hand guides the Bokken's direction.

LEFT HAND - POWER

RIGHT HAND - DIRECTION GUIDE

Checking the Bokken's Curve

Perform the basic Bokken cut whilst standing alongside a flat wall. The body and Bokken should almost be touching the wall for this exercise. Imagine that the tip of the Bokken has a red marking pen attached. As it moves it scribes out the way that the weapon moves. This line will be dictated naturally by the way the hands and arms operate the Bokken.

The line drawn should be of a smooth arc.

If the line goes inwards and outwards then obviously the arms have been swaying during the cut. This is not a clean, correct cut. Practise so this line becomes and feels smooth and regular. This fluid motion and correct arc will enhance the performance of many basic techniques including that of Ikkyo already mentioned.

The Finish

Once the downward cut (strike) is made with the Bokken it is important that one learns how to bring the weapon to a final stop. In order to gain this feeling, it is suggested that the downward cut is performed without any real speed or power. Remember power and speed may easily be added to a movement that is correct, with a solid base, later on.

As the Bokken reaches its final position, the two hands begin to brake the speed of the action by:

1 The right hand (top) turning inwards
2 The left hand (bottom) turning inwards.

As both hands squeeze and turn inwards, the weapon will come to a halt. To enhance this action practise wringing out a wet towel. Make sure the material is wrapped around in the right manner to allow the hands to turn inwards.

The arms are still very slightly bent. Do not wring the towel out with so much effort that it causes the elbows to lock out. The turning is done with the two hands, not the whole arm.

The Finishing Posture

To create a finishing posture that feels strong and well balanced, practise pushing the hips down and lowering the body weight so it can be felt as if it is being pushed through both feet. Squeeze the toes into the mat, as if ANCHORING down. After practising for a time, the Bokken suburi is executed in one unstoppable motion with this feeling of solidarity snapping into form at the very end.

A Good Finish is as Important as a Good Start

The use of the weapons is to assist in the development of the Tai jutsu. With many aspects of training yet to be understood it can easily be recognised that the need for good posture is carried through all the stages of learning.

Now go back and re-practise the Tai jutsu with an emphasis on the finishes. The attitude created by much repetition of Suburi is now added to the previous working knowledge of that which has been already been implanted. Back to Basics.

The confidence of both mental and physical actions is amplified.

Bokken suburi number two

Bokken suburi number one is performed and from the end of this suburi a thrusting movement may be added on. Practise this thrusting motion on its own and then perform the previous suburi and follow on the feeling of advancing the whole body forward in a confident manner.

Thrusting the Bokken forward

Assume Bokken posture.

Step forward in a straight line with the back foot. Hanmi is now formed with the left foot forward. The tip of the Bokken travels forward as the body is advancing. The two hands on the Bokken turn so the blade edge is in a horizontal line. The blade edge of the Bokken is the part that relates to the sharp cutting edge of a Katana. The right hand on the front of the Bokken turns so that its palm is facing down to the mat.

The Thrusting of the Bokken

It is important to note that the hands operate correctly in respect to the thrusting movement, more so when being executed after an initial cutting movement. In order that the full power of the whole body is transmitted through to the tip of the Bokken directly, the space between the left hand positioned to the rear of the weapon and the body MUST remain the same as the body advances forward as it steps through to make the thrust. By keeping this distance as the body travels forward, it makes sure that the tip of the weapon travels forward also. All too often the body moves forward at a greater speed than the hands and the thrust then has to catch up. It must be noted that if the hands squash up against the body then at some point they must extend out.

Exercise

Position one's partner in front of the Bokken, and take a firm stance. All the partner is required to do is to apply some resistance to the tip of the Bokken to ensure that Nage pushes his body through with maximum efficiency. Nage must drive the body (centre point) forward making sure the space between hands and body does not diminish.

It would be the same as pushing a car. If one attempts to push a car forward and the arms collapse then the body still in motion will naturally catch up to create a situation where the arms are squashed. So by keeping the extension on both arms the transmission of power to the area in question is possible. This same concept applies to Tai-jutsu. If the body travels forward, so must the hands.

JO

***The Action of the Body is Limited
Extension of the Mind is Infinite***

The Jo

Jo is a wooden staff made of either red or white oak, in length approximately 50" and with a diameter of 7/8", the Jo is a most versatile weapon. It can be manoeuvred around the body and transferred between the hands very easily.

The Aikido student learns how to use the staff, each stage of learning helping the next stage, and finally resulting in a better understanding of the Art. This is referred to as Aikijo. The three basic stages of learning the Jo are:

1 **Jo Suburi** - Singular exercise performed alone, as with the Bokken.

2 **Jo Kata** - The singular movements are now combined in a manner to create a pattern of flowing movements. A set sequence of movements.

3 **Jo Waza** - Waza means technique. The tai jutsu is applied via the staff. Nage performs techniques on Uke by using the staff. Nage begins with the staff or at a more advanced stage disarms the weapon from Uke and uses it to apply the tai jutsu. This is known as Jo Dori - Jo taking.

When a high standard of performance is reached with the Jo it begins to be used as an extension of the arms. It almost moulds itself as part of the body and simulates the feeling of being alive. This harmonising of an outside source will help develop the attitude of harmonising with Uke.

An advanced form of Jo practice is called **Kumi jo** - advanced Jo practice done with a partner. Both perform set movements either by attack or defence in relation to one another - almost like a choreographed fight scene.

How to Hold the Jo
1 The Jo is held in left hanmi. Unlike the Bokken which always adopts right hanmi, the Jo, though mainly practised in left posture, also uses right hanmi. After all the Jo can be used equally from both ends, the Bokken cannot. The right hand is positioned on the very end of the staff (rear)

The left hand is at the front at a comfortable distance apart. The Jo is parallel to the ground.

IMPORTANT...

Do not grip the staff as though it is a barbell. It is fairly light in weight.
Hold it firmly so it feels comfortable and there is no muscle tension in
the arms or shoulders.   This relaxed but firm grip allows for rapid
movement and an easy base from which to change the hand positions.

Tai Sabaki with the Jo

It is wise to practise Jo-Tai-Sabaki frequently to gain a comfortable working relationship between the staff and the motion of the body. This is an ideal exercise to practise using the total length of the staff, sliding it through the hands as the body performs tai-sabaki. If attending a class specialising in Jo practice then this is an ideal method to prepare oneself, warm up, and generally feel at ease with the staff, before the lesson commences.

SAFETY NOTE ... make sure the staff has no rough or splintered areas, as the hands will most definitely find these when performing this movement. It is wise to lightly sand one's own Jo, for a good 'feel'.

The basic movement has already been learnt and it remains the same. The only variable is that the hands are now operating the Jo as the body is in motion.

This practice develops good co-ordination with oneself and timing to one's own movements. When the Tai sabaki starts so does the Jo; both keep moving until the Jo and the body halt together.

Jo Suburi

The first suburi is a thrusting movement known as Choku Tsuki (pronounced ski, or zuki depending on the school). Whilst various groups favour their own style of Suburis, the basic characteristics of movement and learning remain the same.

Choku Tsuki

1&2   Assuming Jo posture, the front foot slides forward. This temporarily leaves the back hand behind.

The front hand may slide up the Jo a little as the body advances forward. The rear hand keeping a firm grip. The Jo thrusts forward. The back foot follows in time with the hand so that the whole body is working as one machine to execute the thrust. This means the full power of the body is being pushed through the end of the Jo.

NOTE .... in order that the Jo can be thrust through the front hand, this grip must be light. The power of the thrust is emanating from the body, and travelling from the rear hand (right). The front hand acts as a guide.

3   The finishing posture is strong. Do not lean the body forward to try and add more power to the thrust. Note that the back hand has travelled a little past the start position in order to execute the thrust sufficiently.

IMPORTANT

The rear hand on the Jo must keep a firm grip. Even though this is Suburi practice one must take into account that if a strike were to be made, then if the rear grip were weak, the Jo would not be stable. In contact practice the grip gradually tightens up on impact.

Jo Suburi ... Upper Block A

Starting in Jo posture, this suburi is designed in order to protect oneself from an oncoming high strike to the head.

1 Assume Jo posture.

2 Pull the Jo through the left hand until the left hand is positioned on the end of the Jo. The right hand (back) circles this end of the Jo upwards and forward. The right hand positions itself away from the very end of the Jo, so there is space for the block to take place.

3 The back foot steps forward in co-ordination with the hand motions.

4   The hips turn slightly inwards as the Jo reaches its final position.

In the Mind:
Even though the Suburi is done alone...
Keep the mind active......AWARENESS

Jo Suburi... Upper Block B

This suburi is the same as that previously practised, the only difference being that it is performed from right hanmi as opposed to the normal practice of starting in left hanmi. It is important to remember that the Jo is used from both ends, so it is wise to practise from both stances in order that the Jo has freedom of movement whichever foot is forward.

Jo Kata

If one were to assume that each Jo suburi were an individual link, then putting these links together would create a chain. A Kata can be likened to a chain being a combined set of strong links pieced together in a manner so that they are inseparable. A chain is only as strong as its weakest link, so spend time and effort in performing the suburi to a high standard. Thus the chain will not be broken.

Performing kata will develop the natural flow of the body. It should be performed as though it is one long movement from start to finish, with no full stops. This can only be achieved through concentrated and thoughtful repetition.

To show a specific kata may be confusing as different major schools of Aikido have their own set patterns.

Individual Style (Linking)
Performing Jo Kata naturally, shows the student's own characteristics of movement. Whilst the Suburi may remain identical from student to student and the movements in the kata be the same, the end product may appear unique to each student practising it. Individual body tone and tension allow for their own style to form.

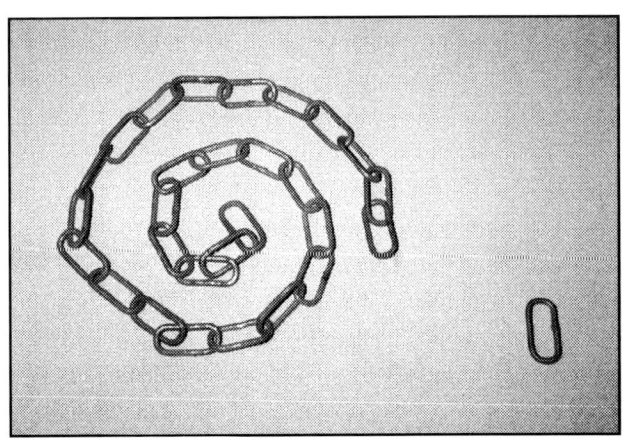

Jo Waza

Nage use the Jo as an extension of the arms, to show Tai-jutsu movements upon Uke. By using the Jo to practise techniques Nage develops a feeling of pushing energy out from the arms throughout the length of the staff and finally throwing Uke. Nage's body movements in relationship to Uke are amplified, allowing one to see some aspects of technique in a clear and uncomplicated way. A sense of Maai is developed.

When one is uninhibited with the movements of the Jo and the performance of technique with Uke, one is able to freely demonstrate the "ART" of Aiki-jo encompassing the following:

a) Nage's individual style and characteristics during movement.
b) The excellence of correct technique applied via the staff.
c) The dynamic use of "Extension" - allowing the vital forces of the body to flow out from the two hands through and beyond Uke.

Jo Waza is also very important for Uke. It will help in the practising of rolls and breakfalling procedures (Ukemi)

Leading Uke - it must be said that whilst Nage has the weapon to begin with, a devastating strike could be made, however the purpose is to lead Uke's intention, not to annihilate.

Basic Starting Position - postures and Maai
1 Nage assumes Jo posture. Uke takes a Gyaku hanmi to Nage. Uke takes the end of the Jo with the leading hand, as if for normal Gyaku hanmi Katatetori.

Important - Uke takes a light grip so Nage may concentrate on the pure movement. EDUCATION FIRST.

The basic principles of Ikkyo are performed, with Nage using the Jo.

1. Uke takes the end of the Jo.
    Nage slides the back foot forward and across, whilst at the same time
    turning the Jo, so it circles up to Uke's face. Keep the leading arm
    extending the body's power out.

2. Nage's back foot steps in deep, becoming the new front foot. Jo
    continuously travelling through Uke, makes Uke turn away. Nage
    advances the whole body, whilst sustaining extension on both arms,
    pushing through the staff.

3. Uke rolls forward once the balance is broken. Nage finishes.

It is important for Nage to see the relationship of how the Ikkyo movement is transferred from the Tai-jutsu practice to the Jo practice. If one looks at photograph 2 with the Jo then it can quite easily be seen how the body positioning of Uke is formed.

Jo Waza Tenchi Nage

Nage and Uke begin on the same line and Uke takes the end of the Jo. This is normal procedure.

1. Stepping first with the front foot and then followed up to make hanmi with the back foot, Nage is positioned off the line. Nage extends the far tip of the Jo down and across to the floor as the body is travelling off line.

Uke must be weak at this stage before moving forward.

2. Nage steps in deep with the rear foot. The back of the Jo travels up and forwards towards Uke's throat. Nage's rear arm and the other arm keep extending outwards as the body advances in. Note this same position in Tai-jutsu practice.

Nage slides the whole body deeper and deeper in and through Uke. Nage remains in the same hanmi as the body travels through. Both arms must be outstretched.

Uke falls to the floor. Nage finishes on a firm posture so as NOT to allow Uke to take him to the ground with him.

Kokyu Nage

The Battle Within Oneself Must Be Conquered
So The Enemy May Pass On By

Kokyu Nage

Kokyu-nage refers to a type of throw that employs no joint technique, thus no painful elements are applied to Uke. Kokyu-nage simply desires Nage to manipulate the energy of the oncoming attack in either of two methods:

1. The attacker's energy is extended in the same direction of the attack, until Uke becomes unbalanced and is thrown.
2. Nage re-directs the attacking energy so that Uke is placed in a position that is unstable and may easily be thrown.

Before one may be competent at performing pure Kokyu-nage, there are two major components that must be looked into, so that Nage is prepared mentally as well as physically. These components can then be applied to what has already been learnt. Go back to the beginning of this book and perform the Tai jutsu again, a new level of understanding energy and force is now brought into focus.

1 How to View the oncoming Attack:

If one's eyes are focused on the weapon then it will be easy for Uke to overpower Nage's mind. If Nage's mind is fixed on the particular weapon, then Uke has taken an advantage and is already mentally dictating that he holds the advantage. Nage must view the situation on his terms.

Look forward in the direction of the opponent.

Do not see a weapon of the closed fist, but see the whole body as the item to be dealt with.

Imagine the attacker as a circular mass of energy. Put a circle around the outline of the body. Now Nage sees the attacker not as an aggressive overpowering force with a deadly weapon, but merely a circular mass of energy, that must be dealt with.

Do not become involved with the attacker's intentions. If one looks into the face of the attacker, it is easy to be mentally unbalanced. The aggressive look and possibly loud unnerving vocabulary acts to amplify Uke's intent. This could lead Nage into feeling weak and that the attacker if far too strong for him to handle.

REMAIN CALM. SEEING A MASS OF ENERGY TRAVELLING TOWARD ME I LEAD IT AWAY.

Kokyu Nage : Extension of Energy Method One

1 Nage and Uke begin on the same line.

2 Uke attacks Yokomenuchi, stepping dominantly forward.

3   Nage raises the leading arm, whilst sliding slightly in with the back foot. The back foot is now the front foot. The amount of energy directed at Nage, determines how much ground this foot has to travel. This will take practice to adjust to the correct Maai during actual motion. It will become an instinct that will be utilised in much of the training. Nage's leading arm is on the inside and top of Uke's attacking arm. Nage keeps Uke's arm travelling in the same direction as its original attacking force by extending the arm.

NOTE... As Nage steps in to keep the attacking force in motion the HIPS and body are off the line of the attack. The hips are slowly beginning to turn.

4   Nage turns on the balls of both feet (as in Shihonage), to face the direction in which Uke is now travelling. Nage's arm that is not controlling the attacking arm of Uke is on its centre line and positioned by Uke's shoulder level as Uke passes by. Both arms are extending continuously as the hips are turning.

5   Nage needs little effort to send Uke on. Nage's hips must be fully turned and the hanmi strong facing Uke as he is thrown.

Practise steadily at first so Uke may have opportunity to roll away safely.

6   **Zanshin -Unbroken Concentration**
This is the follow through of technique, one is connected to one's partner even after the throw. To keep the awareness level at a high standard, Nage must try and remain focused upon Uke even as he rolls away. The main concept of this type of throw is being able to harmonise with not only Uke's body, but Uke's energy. So even though Uke has passed by, remain in unison with the

dispersed energy. This makes Nage's AWARENESS great.

Energy... As already stated it is the attacking force which is being used to throw Uke. This is the Fuel.

The Mechanics are:
Body positioning
Timing
Extension
Attitude

MENTAL TRAINING: If one were to imagine the attacking force as wet concrete, then if it lands on its target it becomes very heavy and solid and difficult to move. Back to Basics Kihon applies. Wet concrete is easy to move, so - if one keeps it from solidifying then it can be moved, around with ease. Fluid form - Ki No Nagare.

Kokyu Nage: Redirection of Energy
Method Two

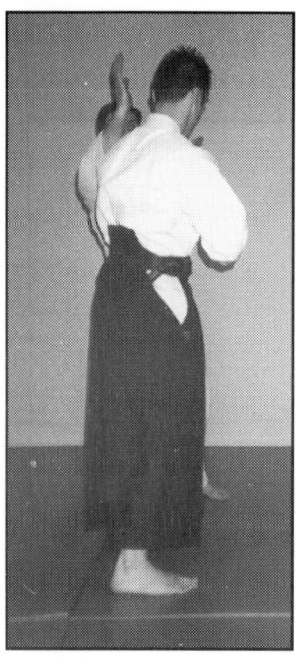

1   Beginning on the same line, Uke attacks Yokomenuchi.

2   Nage raises both hands. The leading hand begins to harmonise with Uke's attacking arm as Nage's back foot slides forward and to the side. It is important that for this particular movement Nage's back foot takes up a new position in line with the existing front foot. The front foot turns on the spot. The hanmi is now being turned to face to the side. During this body movement Nage's leading hand is continuously guiding the attacking energy to the side of Uke. This arm is extended. Nage's free arm guards the centre line at this moment. Uke's balance should be weak as though he seems to be as light as a feather. In time it is acceptable for Nage to slide the whole body further to this side in order to maintain Uke off posture.

3 Both Nage's arms extend out as the hanmi fully turns to face the same direction as Uke is falling. Nage's arm travels from the centre line and helps this motion by guiding Uke's shoulder in this same direction. The body may slide a little further in, this will be done naturally in practice.

In physical motion, Nage's movements are simple... the execution of the throw is largely due to TIMING. Nage must practise so that the strike is intercepted smoothly and extended away with ease. Nage's body moves in a smooth, confident manner from start to finish. If Nage stops, then the energy stops, and so does Uke.

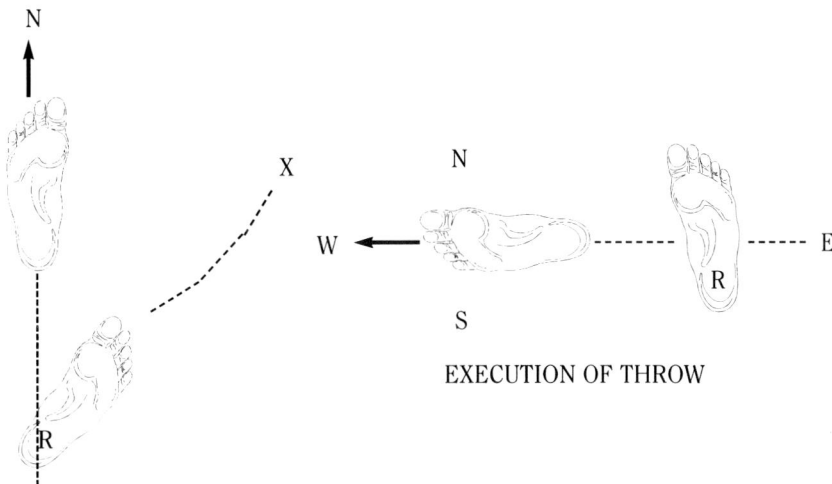

EXECUTION OF THROW

START POSITION

Only two ways of performing Kokyu-nage have been shown, each way illustrating one of the two basic methods of dealing with the oncoming force. There are many different combinations of movements incorporating these methods, some of which involve complex and amplified motions. The essence remains... Timing.

Kokyu

All Aikido techniques, whether it be the simple Tai-jutsu movements or movements with the Jo or Bokken, utilise Kokyu. Kokyu is the evidence of one's breath in motion. In practice we never struggle or use muscular energy to defeat an opponent. When one's breath is in time and matches the opponent's breath, then one's power is unified with the motion of the self and therefore the motions of the attacker. In essence this is harmony. It is a deeper form of harmony than that which has already been studied. To harmonise with the attacker's physical form is naturally important and must be fully understood before one may try and achieve the harmonisation of breath between oneself and the opponent.

As this is a basic text, a Breathing Exercise is explained that may be performed alone and will help in the individual development of kokyu. This exercise may be used as part of the warm-ups and also as a cooling down exercise at the end of practice .

1   Stand in a comfortable manner, this is normally with feet about shoulder width apart. Both feet point forward and remain flat on the ground, the weight is down slightly, which will require both knees to bend. Stay in this position whilst performing the hand movements. Both hands begin in the centre-line position, with both palms facing to the floor. The thumbs and index fingers of both hands are lightly touching.

2   The palms turn upwards and begin to slowly extend. Breathe in through the nose as the hands begin to circle up and out.

3   Time the breathing IN so that when the hands reach this position with the palms facing up, the body is full of air.

At this position, hold the breath. Whilst doing so the palms turn to face the floor.

Breathing OUT through the mouth, the arms begin to slowly travel inwards to the original position.

Finish, then repeat.

It is performed slowly in order that one may breathe in deep and exhale fully. Timing is very important. When the hands start, the breathing starts and when the hands reach the final position, the breath stops. In motion this will be easily recognised.

Keep the shoulders and arms relaxed.........

Look ahead and feel positive. Focus.........

Express the hands fully.............................

Practise again and again. It can be seen how this type of exercise will help Nage with controlling the breath. Nage must try and use this relaxed but sharp focus in the performance of ALL motion.

Breathing and Concentration

These same principles of concentration can be used for all aspects of training, e.g.... Performing suburi, Kokyu exercises.

Sitting Comfortably.
Either sit on the mat or, if it is more comfortable to begin with, upright on a chair.

As you BREATHE IN through the nose, say in the mind the word **IN**. Without actually speaking out loud, the brain hears **IN**. Visualise in the mind, in large letters, the word **IN**.
This boosts concentration, as the action of breathing in is amplified both visually and orally. By performing these tasks, the mind is kept focused on one item, and that is the simple action of breathing in. There is no way the mind may wander off course, using all the senses in unison.
The same system applies when breathing out. **OUT**.

Perform slowly. This is almost a light state of meditation. The brain is allowed to rest from its high intensity of activity. This brings a feeling of calmness to the mind and body.

Expertise

*Excellence In Combat
Is Harmony In Nature*

Expertise

The final point of the star. Once the five points of the star are joined, the outer circle is completed. As a three dimensional shape the star may rotate within its own sphere of harmony.

Expertise is being competent at performing the correct action (even if this is simply exiting the situation) to the oncoming attack. Different situations require different solutions. As a martial artist, with highly developed skills, one has many options of how to deal with a particular instance. It is keeping these skills and options open and available for possible use, if they should ever be needed, that allows one the sense of well-being and overall peace of mind to pursue other avenues in life.

In classroom training, like practising the set patterns of technique and movements within this book, one is in a safe and relaxed environment. One's mental attitude and feeling will be obviously geared to this environment, as this is the best way for learning. One does not accumulate knowledge if one is pressured through fear. It must be noted that in an actual real life predicament both the physical and mental stimuli have changed. By looking at this area one is able to gain and pre-conceive some of the feelings that may be brought to the surface when under these influences.

The Confrontation
When the body is under stress, with the fear of actual combat it becomes influenced by the primitive reflex called "The Fear Reflex". Simply put, this translates as the "fight or flight" response. The pending physical engagement will cause emotional and biological changes. The adrenalin levels will increase and the senses will become very alert. The instinct may be to stand and fight or to exit the situation if this is necessary. This manual has maintained that whilst learning the mechanics and ideals of Aikido one must always be aware of self defence, or more dramatically self-survival aspects of this discipline. Under stress the mind must be focused into processing the right thought responses. There are two parts to this equation. Firstly the most common form of physical engagement and response will be looked at:

I AM ATTACKED --------------- I WILL DEFEND MYSELF
I have the right to defend myself, using the necessary force.

This is the basic thought pattern to channel the brain into action.
The next equation is slightly more open to personal attitude and requires more experience to understand sufficiently well, in order to make the decision for a response.

MY ATTACKER STANDS READY BEFORE ME

Without actually launching an assault, the aggressor confronts his victim, goading him into making a move. If the aggressor has a knife then it can be easy for him to keep pushing and pushing the victim into a position whereby he cannot turn and walk away but must face the inevitable. If as the defender one feels that the situation is getting out of hand then it is time to take control. This is known as "Initiating the Move". It is worth remembering that all the time one is backing away from the aggressor, the aggressor starts to dominate the situation, gaining an advantage - unless one has the experience of inducing this affect to the assailant in order to lure him into a false sense of security before he is dealt with. The sheer unexpectedness of taking control will destroy an opponent's physical and mental balance.

Initiating the Move - Taking Control
This term simply means one takes charge of the situation, by inducing the inevitable combat. One gains the advantage by taking control. The situation is now governed on one's own terms. In order to be competent at performing the specific skills and thought processes adequately, some training exercises are given that will enhance overall performance and enhance the development of:
Reflexes
Timing
Adapting techniques spontaneously
Vision
Awareness
Confidence

Method One

Reflex Training
What is a Reflex Action?
A reflex action is an action which is carried out instantly upon certain types of stimuli, without prior thinking. Example: When the hand accidentally touches a hot iron which has been left on unexpectedly, it pulls itself away automatically. This is a reflex action. The mind does not

think 'What shall I do?' because this would take too long, the body instincts and natural reactions perform the required actions immediately.

If one takes a look back at the Yokomenuchi initial defence procedure it can be seen how the nearest arm to the attacker's blow rises up to protect oneself. This follows a similar reflex/natural reaction. It is a basic survival instinct to put up one's arms if someone is raining blows down upon the head. Using natural movements allows the panic reaction of covering the head with the arms to be skilfully manipulated into this martial arts defences.

Reflex Training Exercise/ How to Take Control - Initiating

This following exercise acts both to educate the way in which one may take charge of a potential assailant and also acts as a way in which to sharpen up one's reflexive skills.

Exercise:

Stand in front of your partner. Raise one hand to tap your partner on the head. Attempt to make a light tap. This can be done lightly with great speed. Practise safely to avoid poking your training partner in the eyes. This acts as a good focusing exercise as well. Your partner simply desires to raise his nearest arm (as though raising the Jo or Bokken) to deflect/ward off the tap to the head. The result will be that either your hand reaches the target with a light touch, or your partner has protected himself so that it has missed. Start the exercise again. To start easily decide with your partner which hand you will be attacking with, so to give him more chance of defence. When this has been practised a while then either hand may be used. Vary the Maai at the start, sometimes close range other times take a step forward. All variables on the attack will help with the defence becoming harmonious and not just the identical response every time.

Taking Charge:

In order to make the first move and begin controlling the situation one must start to dominate the space. Attempt, as before to touch the partner's head. This time however it is done with the edge of the hand as if to make a firm blow to your aggressor's head (Shomenuchi). The aggressor will have two choices at this time. Either he will do nothing and so will be hit, or will raise his arm up to protect himself, as has already been practised. As this is a natural reaction to put up one's hands then it is very likely that this will occur. It is from this position that one begins to execute technique. The raised arm is ideal to perform Ikkyo. It will be easy from this position because the initial part of the Ikkyo technique has been done. Take a firm control of this exposed elbow and wrist and without any hesitation perform a strong non stop Ikkyo motion.

As both a practice of taking control of the situation and a reflex exercise using the tap method of contact is ample in both cases.

Method Two

One on One Practice

This form of intense practice is for two students who wish to feel the progression of their Aikido in motion. Nage allows Uke the freedom to attack in any of the three following ways:

Punch

Yokomenuchi

Double Jacket Grab

Nage's awareness levels must now start to become reflexive. It must be distinguished how the different attacks are coming in, for Nage to correspond accordingly.

Remember to keep to the First Objective: move and defend oneself is the initial concern. Looking good and executing large complex technique is all very well but not to the sacrifice of being hit. As before with the solution to the equation "I will defend myself" if in any doubt of "What will I do" then the programming for this is to simply say to yourself "I Will Move"

I AM ATTACKED ------------- I WILL DEFEND MYSELF
WHAT TO DO ---------------------- MOVE

Movement will allow enough time and space in order to establish control. In a panic attack if the brain is programmed to come up with the answer MOVE that is exactly what one will do.

Never attempt to prearrange what technique should be done when the attacker comes in. There will be enough fear and confusion in the mind without pre-deciding techniques. Besides there would probably not be enough time in the circumstance to do this anyway.

To begin with, agree with Uke to attack focused but at a reduced speed. If one learns to move correctly and safely to begin with then these habits will speed up accordingly as Uke's attacks become harder and faster.

Method Three

Four Ukes.

Awareness Exercise.

Nage must be able to see the attack (At basic Level), and the eyes must be aware of the surroundings. In practice Uke is normally positioned directly in front of Nage, but in reality the attack may come from one's left side or one's right side. The following exercise is designed to make Nage's vision capable of deciphering the direction of the attack and thereafter dealing with the situation. Being able to see both to the front and the sides whilst looking forward one uses peripheral vision, seeing all the surroundings, not just a fixed area.

Nage has four Ukes standing in front, on the same line but spread out. Agree an attack. All four Ukes attack the same to start with, later on in more advanced forms of practice each Uke may attack differently, keeping Nage even more on his toes. As Nage stands in front of the four attackers, with the eyes not fixed upon one particular person, but on the whole of the line, Nage waits calmly to be tested.

Position someone behind Nage to act as pointer. This person points discreetly (so Nage cannot see) to one of the Ukes. This Uke attacks Nage in the agreed form. Sometimes it makes it easier for the pointer to be standing on a chair, behind Nage.

In late forms of practice, at an advanced level the Ukes may begin not on a straight one but in an arched line facing Nage, almost crowding their space.

It is important that Nage remains calm when not being attacked. The time spent motionless as Nage remains on the spot is training in itself. Try not to calculate which Uke has the most probable chance of being picked next, simply view the situation and act as is needed. On paper this sounds very easy, but in practice only time and good concentrated practice will win through. Once the body has inner calmness whilst stationary, then this feeling will be able to be introduced into a violent atmosphere whereby someone desires to do you real damage. Remaining calm, one has open options.

It is also an act of expertise to know when to "Do Nothing" and Walk. At the beginning it was said that Aikido is for self-defence not EGO. Martial Expertise will only be achieved when Nage has taken into account the following guidelines:

Practise with the right spirit. The correct mental attitude is as vital for progress as is the correct physical attitude.

Practise Slowly. Practise Hard. Practise Fast. Practise Soft. All forms of practice develop good Aikido. The body is allowed to change with its mood. Not every day does one have the capabilities of training till one drops, so rather than not train at all the following day, train soft etc.....

Seek more knowledge through a good instructor. Have respect for your Master, as your Master will have for a good student. Respect your Uke. One cannot perform with out one (Tai-Jutsu).

Respect Yourself.

Aikido for Children

Like all the other major martial art groups Aikido is quickly becoming an activity in which children are showing an interest. So much so that classes catering for their special needs are growing in number and size. The majority of Aikido centres now have children's classes ranging from ages 7 to 13 years. Children learn better and with more ease amongst their own peer group, rather than attending adult classes. Obviously there are certain techniques that are not taught to minors for safety reasons. The development of young bones and tissue continues and so must be left undisturbed for natural growth to occur. Applying joint locks to such areas may cause injury either now or later on in the child's development. There is much to learn within Aikido's structure without executing painful locks upon each other at such an early age. The juniors have a love for throwing techniques which involves wholesome body contact and learning to fall correctly becomes enjoyable.

As well as the beneficial elements of children learning how to defend themselves, they also learn how to work and get on with each other whilst becoming healthier and fitter. Learning these physical and social skills will stand any youngster in good stead for life.

Glossary

Stances

Hanmi	- Triangular stance
Ai hanmi	- When the partners are facing each other in the same hanmi (both with the same foot forward)
Gyaku hanmi	- When the partners stand in opposite hanmi to each other, one left foot forward, the other right.
Kiba-dachi	- A straddle leg stance where the body weight is evenly distributed over the feet that are spaced twice the width of the shoulders.

Attacks

Katatetori	- One handed wrist grab
Katatori	- Lapel or shoulder grab
Morotetori	- Two handed forearm grab
Ryokatatori	- Two handed jacket grab
Tsuki	- Thrust/punch
Shomenuchi	- Strike to the centre of the head
Yokomenuchi	- Strike to the side of the head

Persons

Sensei	- Teacher/Instructor
Aikidoka	- Student of Aikido
Nage	- Person executing the technique - the defender
Uke	- Person who receives the technique - the attacker

Body Movements

Tenkan	- Pivot on the front foot
Tai sabaki	- Body movement
Tai no henko	- Body blending exercise

Techniques in this book:

Irimi nage	- Entering body throw
Ikkyo	- Elbow controlling technique
Nikkyo	- Wrist locking technique
Tenchi nage	- A type of throw breaking Uke's balance
Shihonage	- A sword swinging motion applied on the arm
Kotegaeshi	- Small wrist turning technique

Aikido Weaponry

Jo	- Wooden Staff
Bokken	- Wooden Sword
Suburi	- Singular exercises performed with the Jo/Bokken
Kata	- Movements joined in order to create a pattern/flow
Jo Waza	- Technique applied using the staff